# *Descriptive Botanical Terms Illustrated*

P9-EER-859

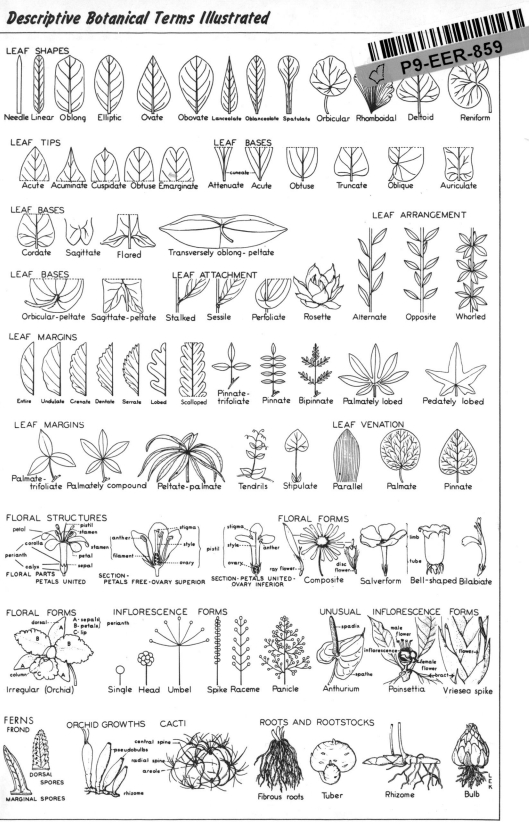

# EXOTIC HOUSE PLANTS

## *Illustrated*

## All the Best in Indoor Plants

by Alfred Byrd Graf

*A Mini-Cyclopedia*
*of House and Decorator Plants.*

*1200 Photographs*

*Each with Pictograph*

*to Requirements,*

*Care and Use*

# 8th
**EDITION**

# ROEHRS COMPANY - *Publishers*
East Rutherford, New Jersey 07073, U. S. A.

# Contents

International Standard
Book Number
ISBN 0–911266–07–0

Library of Congress
Card No. 72–97182

© Copyright 1973
by A. B. Graf

Printed in U.S.A.

Art Director:
Norman E. Carley

Lithography:
DeVries Brothers, N. J.

Bindery:
A. Horowitz & Son, N. J.

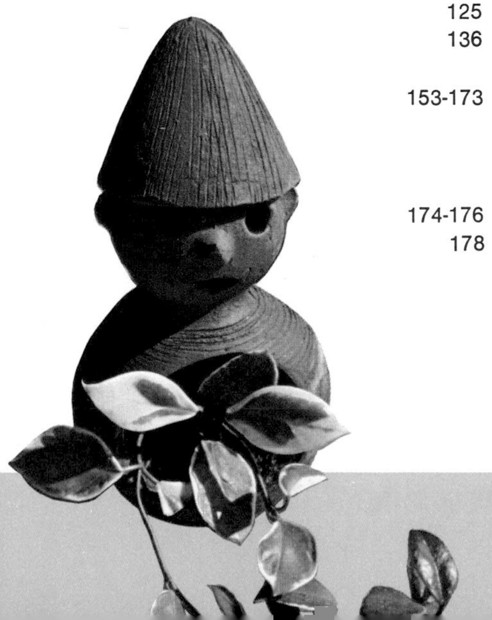

*our Exótico Chiquito with
Hoya carnosa 'Tricolor',
the "Krimson Queen" wax vine*

Tropical Plants in Terracotta Bowl: (from bottom left, clockwise) Dracaena goldieana, Dracaena sanderiana, Nepenthes x atrosanguinea, Anthurium andraeanum album and andraeanum, Xanthosoma lindenii 'Magnificum', Hoffmannia ghiesbreghtii, Aglaonema costatum; as ground covers Ficus radicans 'Variegata', Selaginella kraussiana brownii, Peperomia obtusifolia variegata.

# Exotic House Plants— an Introduction

This Illustrated Mini-Cyclopedia presents a complete pictorial survey of all basic indoor plants, brought together to serve every purpose. The 1200 plants selected represent a diversified and interesting collection to choose from, tested by horticulture and experience, and proven as suitable for the living room, office decoration, home greenhouse or, in warmer environment, the patio outdoors.

Plants have been grouped into 18 categories according to their characteristics or affinities, as a visual aid to pursue any special decorative scheme, or collector's hobby. The implementary descriptive text for each plant lists the scientific name, its family affinity, native homeland, and vernacular name, followed by brief details on foliage and flower colors or other specific characters. Where vital measurements are stated these are in International metrics. Shown with each plant photo is an easy-to-understand pictograph symbol, fully explained on pages 10–11 and each indicating preferred environment and growing needs in Temperature, Location, Light, Soil and Moisture.

Botanical names are based principally on such standard works as Bailey's "Hortus" and "Manual of Cultivated Plants", the "Royal Horticultural Dictionary of Gardening", "Parey's Blumengaertnerei", and "Engler's Pflanzenreich", as well as my own cyclopedia "Exotica". Nomenclature has further been constantly guided by the latest findings of the Bailey Hortorium of Cornell University, the National Herbarium in Washington, and professional reports internationally. A listing of American vernacular names should prove helpful to those less familiar with scientific names.

Since a world-wide collection of tropical and subtropical exotics has been maintained by the Roehrs Company for more than a century, I have been fortunate to be able to personally observe and to photograph the plants shown in this book, as growing in our many greenhouses. In addition, many of my photos were taken during my life-long travels into all the tropical and subtropic regions of the world. There I have visited collections of exotica, and on expedition studied floristic habitats in all the Americas; across Africa, to Malaysia, the South Pacific and Australia; the West Indies and the East Indies, from Chile to Japan, from Guinea to New Guinea, from Leningrad to Cape Town. To be acquainted with climatic backgrounds in these areas points the way to the conditions under which our plants best wish to live.

EIGHTH EDITION 1973: Since first published in 1953, succeeding printings have primarily endeavoured to make revisions according to latest nomenclatural findings. This new 8th edition, however, is intended also to reflect the changes of the past 20 years, by plants newly introduced or cultivated, as well as to utilize the better quality of photographs which I have taken during more recent times. Consequently, all plant photos are entirely new, including many additions not previously pictured.

It has been my earnest purpose to bring together as complete a collection as possible of the various types of recommended indoor plants in this pictorial handbook. In so doing I hope to be able to share the pleasure of a lifetime of experience amongst plants with everyone cherishing nature for its ever-changing charms and beauty.

8th Edition May 1973

Alfred B. Graf

*Covered peristyle of the interior court of a suburban residence in Westchester, New York. Ideally suited for naturalistic planting with attractive and colorful exotic plants, and West Indian treeferns (Cyathea arborea) for tropical accent, the area features a pool and flagstone walks as well as a patio area for dining and restful reading. Roofing of frosted glass admits diffused light, and the plants are thriving in each other's company under optimum conditions of humidity and temperature.*

# Tropical Beauty to live with

Exotic plants from warm, frost-free regions are brought into home or office, established in pots or tubs, primarily in climates with freezing winters. They have become an integral part of our modern concept of everyday life, adding fresh beauty and living charm all year. Man's impulse moves him toward living with nature, and to transplant its greenery and allure indoors. A little corner in your room or office, under lamp or near the window, is not only ideal for the long life of a house plant, but adds a spot of color and decor to furnishings. A glassed-in porch is fine for cooler subjects and light-hungry flowering plants, while a little home greenhouse, or even a glass terrarium, would provide the humid-warm conditions required by the more dainty tropicals, and many ferns.

Those plants that adjust best to comfortable room temperatures are usually denizens of the tropics and near-tropics, or cultivars derived from them. Dwellers in cold climate regions are intrigued because of their appeal in an exotic manner. In an awareness of their being quite motile, they become objects of tender affection when cultivated as a house plant. Doing so will not only tend to embellish any area of the home, but its recuperative therapy rewards the indoor gardener by relaxing his tensions, and contributing to his ultimate well-being.

A choice group of colorful foliage plants is more than just a decoration that must be worried over, and watered at regular times—they are a gathering of living beings, and each can tell a story of its exotic homeland. Their very behavior reminds us that they are full of life—they may be neglected and sad and need attention, or they can repay you with exuberance in gratitude for your care.

**TOP SHELF, LEFT TO RIGHT:**

Cryptanthus bromelioides tricolor
Kalanchoe tomentosa
Acalypha hispida
Fittonia verschaffeltii argyroneura
Anthurium warocqueanum
Piper porphyrophyllum
Calathea makoyana
Hedera helix 'Maculata'
Vriesea splendens 'Major'
Anoectochilus roxburghii
Anthurium scherzerianum

on opposite page

**SECOND SHELF:**

Iresine lindenii formosa
Hedera canariensis fa. arborescens
Ficus radicans 'Variegata'
Begonia masoniana ('Iron Cross')
Homalomena wallisii
Syngonium wendlandii
Maranta leuconeura massangeana
Philodendron ilsemannii
Peperomia verschaffeltii
Ficus rubiginosa variegata

**THIRD SHELF:**

Pleomele reflexa variegata
Bougainvillea 'Harrisii'
Aphelandra fascinator

Aglaonema 'Pseudobracteatum'
Aphelandra aurantiaca
Chamaeranthemum igneum
Ananas comosus variegatus
Sinningia regina
Begonia boweri
Cordyline terminalis 'Baby Ti'

**BOTTOM SHELF:**

Osmanthus heterophyllus variegatus
Costus sanguineus
Scindapsus aureus 'Marble Queen'
Codiaeum (Croton) 'Duke of Windsor'
Episcia cupreata 'Frosty'
Dieffenbachia 'Exotica' ('Arvida')
Begonia rex 'Merry Christmas',
Dracaena sanderiana

# How to Care for Plants Indoors

The requirements for growth of any plant are: temperature, light, water, and plant nutrients. The latter may be said to include carbon dioxide of the atmosphere, but since this is rarely lacking, we need not usually worry about it. Nutrients lead us to the soil problem, but plants are quite adaptable to most mixes that happen to be available.

The matter of light and temperature requirement has much to do with the class of the plant. Exotics generally come from warm countries, and we are prone to think of them as requiring really torrid temperatures, but surprisingly they generally do best in rooms which we would term cool or downright cold, such as a poorly heated glass-enclosed porch. The benefits of cooler nights are needed for the translocation of manufactured sugars from the leaves to the roots and other growing parts of the plant.

The key to the problem is water, the medium for life, which constitutes about 90% of the plant's make-up, and carries its food supply. Water is absorbed through the roots and is transpired through the green parts. The rate of absorption depends on the root system and the soil, and the size and nature of the container.

We have no difficulty in imagining the sides of a tropical canyon next to a waterfall, clothed with delicate foliage, jewelled with drops of spray. Here the air has no drying power, it is saturated with moisture, its humidity is 100%. The beautiful plants flourishing in this habitat are creatures of just such atmospheric humidity. Take them into a well-heated living room where the air carries only a small fraction of the moisture it can hold, and evaporation far outruns the capacity of the plant to replace the loss of moisture. Wilting, drying out, and death of the plant easily follow. This is the unfortunate history of many plants injudiciously or thoughtlessly brought into the home.

However, from xerophytic regions with little moisture come plants that are invulnerable to drought, and from tropical undergrowth come others tolerant of gloom, some of which show remarkable adjustment to living room conditions. From these classes, with thousands of varieties, by experiment and experience, are selected popular house plants, varying with locality, climate and fashion.

## Light is Vital

Light cannot be measured for its intensity alone, but growth or flowering is usually regulated by length of day or night. The metabolism of a plant—its rate of growth—is in direct relation not only to temperature but also the quality and duration of light received. During fall and winter when the days are short and temperature is low, growth virtually ceases. Most plants will not bloom unless the intensity of light approximates that in their native habitat. Foliage plants are quite tolerant of low light intensity, but if the environment of a flowering plant is too dark, sufficient supplementary light must be provided for successful blooming; a sunny window or an incandescent spotlight is usually best. Many flowering plants are sensitive to daylength, and this is known as photoperiodism. Long day (short night) as well as short day (long night) plants can be guided into blooming practically at will. By giving additional hours of artificial light on short days to long-day plants as Gardenias, Calceolarias and many spring flowering annuals, early flowering is induced. Covering short-day plants such as Chrysanthemums with a black cloth for several hours when the days are long will bring them into bloom as their blooming is dependent on day-length as well as temperature. Intermittent light applied during the night is as effective as continuous light, in obtaining short night response in plants.

## The Influence of Temperature

Plant activities and growth generally increase with higher temperatures, and are retarded if the temperature is low. However, excessive heat may result in injury from desiccation and a rate of respiration so high that the consumption of food materials tends to exceed production by photosynthesis. If temperatures are steadily too high, the plant uses up the stored food manufactured during daytime and may exhaust itself, unless followed by an alternate period of lower temperature to restore its energy. Temperature affects growth through its influence upon all metabolic activities: photosynthesis, respiration, digestion, transpiration, absorption of water, and root growth.

*Self-watering devices for the home: left— an Aphelandra louisae standing on a saucer and placed inside a transparent polythene plastic bag which will condense and conserve moisture for weeks. Right—a Dieffenbachia 'Rud. Roehrs' drawing water by capillarity through a spun-glass wick from a nearby pitcher.*

*A windowsill in a modern German home that really invites house plants: a plate of polished black marble extends the full width of the living room, the heat radiator underneath. Airy windows and gauzy curtains for optimum light combine to provide near greenhouse conditions for almost anything in pots.*

## Soil Moisture

Soil moisture should be evenly maintained. Water a pot when the surface begins to get dry. Generally, plants with coarse roots and growing in heavier, loamy soil should be allowed to get on the dry side, then water well by thoroughly soaking the pot. But root-balls full of very fine fibrous roots, and growing in humusy soil mix, must be kept more evenly moist. To determine the moisture condition simply "feel" the soil; if it feels dry and hard to the touch, and it looks light-colored, then it is high time to water; if the soil feels damp or muddy, and looks dark, then better wait a day or longer. Generally, more watering is required in a heated room during winter time, possibly daily, while in summer, when the radiators are off, watering two or three times a week may be sufficient. No plant should stand for long in water unless a water plant, or is suitable for hydroponic culture.

## Soils and Feeding

The selection of a proper soil mix for any given plant is not as important as many specific recommendations would make it seem. Proof of this is found in the fact that based on University of California experiments, a universal mix could well be recommended for nearly all plants, consisting of equal parts of peatmoss with fine sand. Such a mix would of course have to be enriched by fertilizer because it would be lacking in basic plant food. But in areas with good garden soils fancy trimmings are not necessary as friable loam mixed with some humus will suit most any house plant satisfactorily. Eastern experiment stations recommend a basic mix of 1 loam, 1 peatmoss, and 1 pebbly perlite. Remember that the more delicate-fragile exotics with hairfine fibrous roots will want the addition of more humusy soil, leafmold, peatmoss, sphagnum, shredded fir-back or humus-compost with sand or perlite for drainage. Such soils have the advantage of not needing as a rule, the addition of much plant food, as the decomposing organic matter will provide for average needs. A bit of rotted barn manure or fish fertilizer for nitrogen, and possibly a little ground bone to add phosphate, will be of long-lasting benefit. One should not worry so much about when and what to feed a plant, as this is often over-emphasized.

## Propagation

Home propagation of house plants is often not difficult. Those plants that branch from the base or make suckers can be multiplied by division. Most other plants are propagated by tip cuttings, using half-ripened tops or branches. An age-old practice is to root these in a glass or jar with an inch or two of water, or insert the cutting in a pot or box with sand or peat-perlite mix, water well, and cover for two or three weeks with plastic to make an airtight, moisture holding tent. Raising plants from seed may be necessary for annuals, however, takes longer for most house plants than cuttings but it can be fun.

*This small sand box is a miniature propagating house for cuttings with its effective moisture-confining tent of thin plastic.*

# Plants for Sunny and for Shady Windows

For Gardening indoors the window is best. Not only is natural daylight better than artificial light, but the exposure from different directions offers an ideal place for almost any type of plant. Four simulated windows show what can be used and where.

Seldom, however, are all four sides in a home equally available and suitable for plants. But the suggested types offer the opportunity to make a wise selection for any window. This should not, however, prevent us from trying any plant in whatever spot that may happen to be otherwise ideal. A north window can, if necessary, be artificially lighted, and a south window easily shaded.

For ease of care, attractive looks, and flourishing growth of plants try grouping them in boxes. For convenient access to the window, these could be mounted on legs with rollers. Fill a window box with moist peatmoss, and plunge your pots rim-deep. If the peatmoss is kept moist, plants absorb by capillary action, whatever they may need and practically take care of themselves, though some pots may have to be watered individually on occasion. The roots begin to ramble, and the big plants and the little ones, the climbers and the creepers, flowering plants and foliage together form a mutually beneficial ecology with a microclimate that favors luxuriant, natural growth. In close symbiosis, they enjoy each other's company, and will soon create the image of a natural tropic mini-landscape, cover the other's blemishes, and sickly plants take on new life. Miraculously, plants begin to flower, and even delicate exotics seem to forget their being super-sensitive. The secret lies in the complementary give-and-take and intimate climate set up by such an harmonious community of partners, and a window filled with beautiful exotics brings both restfulness and life into the home.

*(handwritten margin note: mixture of complementary plants in window boxes enhances growth — must try)*

**NORTH WINDOW**  *(Sunny day in winter near glass, 150–500 footcandles; average 300 fc).*

Sun-less windows are not for most flowering plants. But foliage plants including tender tropicals do well in a fully light north window. Weather-stripping or a protective sheet of plastic to prevent cold drafts is advisable during the cold season. A recommended list of satisfactory subjects would be:

For WARM conditions—Aroids such as Aglaonema, Dieffenbachia, Philodendron, Scindapsus and Syngoniums; Cissus, Dichorisandra, Dizygotheca, Dracaenas; ferns including Platycerium; Ficus elastica and lyrata; Fittonias, Hoffmannias, Marantas, Peperomias and Pileas; even Sansevierias.

For INTERMEDIATE temperatures—Amomum, Araucaria, Aspidistra, spider plants (Chlorophytum), hollyferns (Cyrtomium), Helxine, Saxifraga, Tolmiea, Tradescantias; also most palms including Kentias (Howeia).

At a COLD window—Ardisia, Fatshedera, Fatsia (Aralia), Laurus, Ophiopogon, Rohdea and Skimmia; also all kinds of ivies (Hedera helix).

**SOUTH WINDOW**

*(Midday sun, near glass 5500 fc winter, to 8000 fc summer; cloudy day 1000–2000 fc).*

An exposure to the potent southern sun offers a wonderful chance to grow the many plants that are sun-lovers. This includes practically all the holiday blooming plants; flowering shrubs and vines; miniature subtropical fruit trees; many bulbs; and of course the exciting world of succulents.

Plants responding to both sun and WARMTH are—Acalyphas and Croton; Achyranthes, Coleus and Iresine; Amaryllis and other tropical bulbs; Beloperone, Gardenia, Hibiscus and Strelitzia; Tropical clamberers such as Allamanda, Bougainvillea, Clerodendrum, Gloriosa, Jasmine, and Passiflora; flowering succulents like Euphorbia splendens and pulcherrima (Poinsettia), and Kalanchoe; also sunny Dendrobium and Oncidium orchids.

INTERMEDIATE and COOLER plants in need of sun but with the window open when it is warm outside—are Abutilon, Campanula isophylla, and most bedding stock; Geraniums, Petunias, wax begonias, Lantanas; Azaleas, Chrysanthemums, heather, Hydrangeas, Pot roses; Lachenalia and Veltheimia, also Dutch bulbs; fruited Jerusalem cherry; Kumquats and other Citrus.

Most cacti and other succulents enjoy the sun; want to be warm in daytime but cool at night.

**EAST or WEST WINDOWS**

*(Winter sun, near glass, 2000–4000 fc, off-sun 200–500 fc; average 2000 fc).*

The partial sunshine of several hours daily at an East or West window is ideal for many flowering and foliage plants that normally grow in partial shade and dislike the intense sun of windows facing South. East windows are generally cooler and receive the clear morning sun; Western exposures tend to be warmer but often with hazy or moderated light.

WARM PLANTS doing well East or West with the benefit of a limited amount of sun are— Anthurium scherzerianum, Alpinia, Aphelandra, Brassaia, Brunfelsia, Caladium, Calathea, Clivia, Costus, Eucharis; Birdsnest and Boston ferns; Ficus benjamina, Hoyas, Impatiens, Jacobinia, oleander, Pandanus, Pseuderanthemum, Spathiphyllum, Torenia, Zebrinas. Great variety is also offered in the many Begonias, bromeliads, and warm orchids. More or less hairy gesneriads, such as African violets (Saintpaulia), Achimenes, Aeschynanthus, Columneas, gloxinias, Rechsteinerias, Smithianthas, and Streptocarpus enjoy the good light East or West but in sunny hours this light must be diffused to prevent burning.

INTERMEDIATE or COOLER PLANTS for partial sun are—Araucaria, Aucuba, Asparagus, Camellias, Cinerarias, Crinum, Cyclamen, Euonymus, Fuchsia, Grevillea, Kaempferia, Marica, Myrtus, Osmanthus, Oxalis, Plectranthus, Podocarpus, Primula, Vinca, and variegated ivies.

# Light and its Importance to Plants

Northward for shade plants *(protect from chills)*: *(top)* Guzmania musaica; *(center)* Maranta leuconeura massangeana, Spathiphyllum floribundum, Ficus radicans 'Variegata', Begonia masoniana, Hoya carnosa variegata, Begonia rex 'Peace', Anthurium crystallinum, Philodendron squamiferum, Dieffenbachia picta 'Rud. Roehrs'; *(bottom)* Maranta leuconeura kerchoveana, Cryptanthus zonatus zebrinus, Scindapsus aureus 'Marble Queen', Fittonia verschaffeltii argyroneura, Calathea makoyana.

Southern exposure for sun-lovers: *(top)* Cotyledon undulata, Gymnocalycium mihanovichii friederickii, Kalanchoe marmorata, Opuntia microdasys, Pachyphytum 'Blue Haze', Haworthia margaritifera; *(center)* Aeonium haworthii, Euphorbia lactea cristata, Crassula 'Tricolor Jade', Sansevieria 'Hahnii', Cephalocereus senilis, Echeveria glauca pumila, Ananas comosus variegatus, Vriesea carinata; *(bottom)* Aechmea fasciata, Opuntia ficus-indica 'Burbank's Spineless', Echeveria 'Setoliver', Kalanchoe tomentosa, Mammillaria geminispina, Echinocereus dasyacanthus, Kalanchoe daigremontiana hybrid, Espostoa lanata, Crassula rupestris, Sansevieria trifasciata 'Golden hahnii', Cereus 'Peruvianus hybrid' *(specimen)*, x Gastrolea 'Spotted Beauty'.

East for cool morning sun: *(top)* Hedera helix 'Manda's Star', Hedera helix 'Manda's Crested'; *(center)* Begonia semperflorens; *(bottom)* Ficus elastica 'Decora', Hedera helix 'Hahn's Variegated', Dracaena marginata, Hedera canariensis 'Variegata', Euonymus japonicus medio-pictus, albo-marginata, microphyllus variegata; Eurya japonica 'Variegata', Dracaena godseffiana, Cissus antarctica.

Moderate Western light- *warm and diffused:* *(top)* Episcia cupreata 'Acajou', Saintpaulia ionantha hybrid, Howeia forsteriana, Episcia reptans 'Lady Lou', Syngonium wendlandii; *(bottom)* Dieffenbachia picta, Philodendron elegans, Peperomia caperata 'Emerald Ripple', Alocasia x amazonica, Calathea zebrina, Aphelandra squarrosa 'Louisae', Campelia zanonia 'Mexican Flag'. Philodendron 'Lynette'.

## *How a CODE to CARE can help*

A key to plant care such as devised for this Manual can at best be only a general guide. Based on the climatic background of our cultivated exotics, the pictograph symbols assigned to each plant try to spell out the conditions prevailing in their native habitats, to provide whatever would make them happiest in the plant lover's care. However, many plants are quite flexible in their requirements and have shown a remarkable capacity for tolerance and adaptation to unfavorable environment. Anyone interested in plants may attempt with confidence their cultivation at home. Many a beginner has succeeded with growing a fancy plant on a window sill which would worry an expert, proving only that the so-dalled "Green thumb" is no miracle gift but merely the result of careful observation and patient understanding of the plant's needs.

This CODE to CARE should be of special help to the amateur gardener. Once having understood and mastered the basic fundamentals there is nothing to prevent the adventurous from trying his own best methods and with a little feeling for the plant he will probably be successful. To grow plants is an art, and not an exact science—yet for this very reason it is so fascinating.

## EXPLANATION OF THE FIVE ELEMENTS COMBINED
## IN THE PICTOGRAPH SYMBOLS USED IN THIS HANDBOOK

### *Environment*

**HOUSE PLANT:** can be used for home and interior decoration, as it tolerates the reduced light of the living room or office with its artificially dry atmosphere.

**GREENHOUSE PLANT:** Requires relative high humidity such as can be maintained in home greenhouse, under plastic shelter, or a glass terrarium.

### *Temperature*

**W** **Warm:** 62–65° F (16–18° C) at night, can rise to 80 or 85° F (27–30° C) in daytime before vents must be opened.

**T** **Temperate:** 50–55° F (10–13° C) at night, rising to 65 or 70° F (18–21° C) on a sunny day or higher with air.

**C** **Cool:** 40–45° F (5–7° C) at night, 55–60° F (13–15° C) when sunny, with air; 50° F (10° C) in cloudy weather.

TEMPERATURE CONVERSION

°F  0   10   20   30   40   50   60   70   80   90  +100

°C      -10          0          10          20        30

Fahrenheit-Centigrade

### *Light*

**Maximum Light** (sunny South window). "Maximum light" plants theoretically have a preference of 4000–8000 footcandles (for average daylength) for growth, but for mere maintenance will tolerate between 500–2000 fc. A South window facing direct sun is ideal.

**Partial Shade** (East or West window). Plants classified "Partial shade" would like 1000–3000 footcandles but will survive at 100–1000 fc. A simple indicator of diffused sunlight is to pass your hand over your plants and barely see its shadow. A clear East or West window is best, but a Southern exposure must be lightly shaded from direct sun by Venetian blinds, a bamboo screen, or curtain. For mere maintenance of most plants in this group in the home, light intensity may go as low as 25 fc.

**Shady** or away from sun (North window). Delicate exotics designated "Shady" are safest in a North window, with diffused light, and would normally receive 50–500 footcandles. There are very few plants which do not want some sunlight by preference; shade lovers are limited mostly to delicate plants from the forest floor, and ferns. Under artificial illumination, light intensity may be as low as 10 fc. High humidity is important to the well-being of plants in this group.

### *Soil*

**Loam, rich garden soil,** or decomposed granite with some rotted manure or some humus; also, in heavy soils add some sand or grit to prevent caking.

**Humusy soil,** rich in organic matter; sphagnum peatmoss is excellent for moisture-holding capacity; also leafmold. Add a small amount of loam; perlite for drainage.

### *Watering*

**Moderately Dry.** Drench thoroughly then allow to dry between waterings. This admits air into the soil structure which, in turn, promotes development of a healthy white root system; wiry, thick roots being characteristic of this group. Watering means soaking the root-ball penetratingly holding the pot if necessary in a bucket, sink or tub of tepid water until air bubbles cease to rise.

**Evenly moist** but not constantly wet. Plants so classified generally have delicate, hair-like, fibrous roots, subject to rot if kept too wet, and equally easily burning and shrivelling if too dry, especially in hot weather. Maintain uniform moisture throughout the root-ball, without letting the soil become water-soaked and "sour".

**PICTOGRAPH SYMBOLS AT BASE OF EACH PHOTO, OR THE NUMBERS
IN THE DESCRIPTIVE TEXT INDICATE PLANT REQUIREMENTS AND TOLERANCE.**

| ADAPTABLE AS HOUSE PLANT | | | | BETTER AS GREENHOUSE PLANT | | |
|---|---|---|---|---|---|---|
| suitable for growing or decoration in Home, Office, or sheltered Patio; tolerates dry atmosphere | | |  | in need of humid or airy conditions; Glass Terrarium or Plastic frame. Not recommended for the living room. | | |
| **WARM** 62–80° F 16–26° C | **TEMPERATE** 50–65° F up 10–18° C | **COOL** 40–60° F up 5–15° C | | **WARM** 62–80° F 16–26° C | **TEMPERATE** 50–65° F up 10–18° C | **COOL** 40–60° F up 5–15° C |

## PLANTS IN LOAMY GARDEN SOIL, HUMUS ADDED

| WARM | TEMP | COOL | Light / Moisture | WARM | TEMP | COOL |
|---|---|---|---|---|---|---|
| W 1 | T 13 | C 25 | **Maximum Light; Sunny** 4,000-8,000 Footcandles KEEP ON DRY SIDE | W 51 | T 63 | C 75 |
| W 2 | T 14 | C 26 | KEEP EVENLY MOIST | W 52 | T 64 | C 76 |
| W 3 | T 15 | C 27 | **Partial Shade; Diffused Sun** 1,000-3,000 Footcandles KEEP ON DRY SIDE | W 53 | T 65 | C 77 |
| W 4 | T 16 | C 28 | KEEP EVENLY MOIST | W 54 | T 66 | C 78 |
| W 5 | T 17 | C 29 | **Shady; Away From Sun** 50-1,000 Footcandles KEEP ON DRY SIDE | W 55 | T 67 | C 79 |
| W 6 | T 18 | C 30 | KEEP EVENLY MOIST | W 56 | T 68 | C 80 |

## HUMUSY; SOIL RICH IN HUMUS; OSMUNDA OR FIRBARK ON EPIPHYTES, SUCH AS ORCHIDS

| WARM | TEMP | COOL | Light / Moisture | WARM | TEMP | COOL |
|---|---|---|---|---|---|---|
| W 7 | T 19 | C 31 | **Maximum Light; Sunny** 4,000-8,000 Footcandles KEEP ON DRY SIDE | W 57 | T 69 | C 81 |
| W 8 | T 20 | C 32 | KEEP EVENLY MOIST | W 58 | T 70 | C 82 |
| W 9 | T 21 | C 33 | **Partial Shade; Diffused Sun** 1,000-3,000 Footcandles KEEP ON DRY SIDE | W 59 | T 71 | C 83 |
| W 10 | T 22 | C 34 | KEEP EVENLY MOIST | W 60 | T 72 | C 84 |
| W 11 | T 23 | C 35 | **Shady; Away From Sun** 50-1,000 Footcandles KEEP ON DRY SIDE | W 61 | T 73 | C 85 |
| W 12 | T 24 | C 36 | KEEP EVENLY MOIST | W 62 | T 74 | C 86 |

*Aphids on Hibiscus*     *Whitefly on Fuchsia*     *Hard shell scale on Erythrina*     *Mealybugs on Butterfly gardenia*

# Watch out for Insect Pests!

Red Spider

Scale

Mealybug

Aphis

White Fly

Mite

## Pest Control

Plants aren't happy when, encouraged by dry atmospheric room conditions, insect pests appear.

1. Aphis, tiny green or black plant-lice, sucking juices around growing tips or underside of leaves.

2. Mealybugs, pinkish crawlers dusted white, hiding under foliage or in leaf axils, often in a white cottony mass.

3. Red Spider, minute spider-like mites on underside of leaves, in time spinning gauzy webs, multiplying rapidly in dry-warm rooms. Causes discoloration of foliage.

4. White Fly, moth-like scales with and without wings. Often on bedding plants, lantanas, geraniums, where they suck juices from underside of foliage.

5. Scale, small, sucking, turtle-shaped or shield-like bodies mostly stationary, usually black or brown; white on ferns.

## Simple Home Control of Pests

House plants should be diligently observed for the possible appearance of insect enemies, and to prevent any population build-up that is difficult to control. Where plants are few, it is good practice to wipe the foliage with a damp cloth to remove possible pests, to keep the breathing pores open, and for cleaner and better appearance. When it becomes necessary, clean or spot-spray for specific problems as they arise. A light spray of rubbing alcohol half diluted with water in a hand atomizer causes any mealybugs present to turn brown. A touch with a cotton-tipped toothpick or artist's brush dipped in alcohol (including whisky) or ether (nailpolish remover) is sure death for a mealybug, scale or aphid, but care must be taken or these concentrates may burn the foliage.

General infestations on house plants can be discouraged by the simple hygienic means of forcefully syringing each plant every week or two with clear water—especially the undersides of leaves. This is best done in sink, bathtub, the shower, or outdoors, and should dislodge any unwanted guests. Washing keeps foliage clean for breathing and a plant more healthy besides.

Some of the old-fashioned home remedies are still useful today. A bath in warm soap suds (2 tablespoons soap flakes or octagon soap in 4 liter (1 gal.) water is a mild remedy for foliage plants. If the plants are large and unwieldy, such a soap solution can be used for washing of the leaves with a sponge or a toothbrush.

Of course, washing with water alone is not always the complete answer if pests should entrench themselves in hiding places of leaf axils, growing tips or in dense foliage. If badly infested, the entire foliage of a plant may be immersed for 30 seconds in a bath of a warm soapy solution containing a teaspoon of nicotine sulphate to each 4 liter of water, and rinsed a few hours later; this should control green or black aphids and scale. Nicotine spray, if not available, can be home-made by soaking tobacco from cigars or from pipe tobacco in water for several days; dilute to the color of weak tea for use.

## Diseases and Other Ailments

Diseases of house plants, generally are not a major problem due to the dry atmosphere in the average home. Powdery MILDEW is caused by fungi which may become a problem with sudden changes in temperature, cold drafts, or dampness. Use one of the spray mixtures containing Karathane with a soapy spreader added to penetrate the waxy powder.

*The tools that can be used to control these and other problems. From left to right a rubber bulb for Fermate dusts or Sulphur to control mildew or plant diseases, also for use of insecticide dusts; a Bronx sprayer-mister with suction pump action; a rust-proof plastic hand-sprayer for mist, with lever action; a push-button-valve aerosol pressure sprayer in metal can filled with a general bug-killer combining pyrethrum, rotenone and petroleum distillate.*

*The modern trend toward decorating indoors or on the patio with specimen exotic evergreens and palms in fancy bowls and jardinieres of highly glazed ceramics or fiberglass brings back memories of the Victorian era of pleasant and relaxed living. Decorative container plants as shown at International Flower Show, New York: background – Dracaena massangeana, Chamaedorea erumpens, Dracaena marginata; center – Araucaria, Chamaerops, Dieffenbachia, Croton; foreground – Scindapsus, Spathiphyllum, Pittosporum, Chamaedorea elegans, Brassaia, Aglaonema.*

## Maintenance of Decorator Plants

Clean foliage improves the appearance of a decorative plant and assists it in maintaining its life processes. To wipe the foliage with soft cloth will cleanse the breathing stomates, and a touch of milk adds luster to the leaves. Commercial leaf-shiners or oils should be used with caution as they may clog the pores or otherwise cause damage. It is safer to dilute leaf-polish up to 50%.

If a plant stands a long time, say a year, in the same pot, and the roots have filled the same to capacity, mild feedings once a month will sufficiently sustain it. It may be more desirable to confine a house plant, intended for decoration, to as nearly as possible its original size by merely "maintaining" it, watering it sparingly and withholding growth-stimulating feeding. Such a plant will subsist on a minimum of care although in the "weaning" process from the humid greenhouse to a relatively dry living room a few leaves may initially drop before the subject becomes adjusted to its new surroundings. But after that, a plant so conditioned will be less troublesome, not always crying for attention, and continue for a long time to grace the spot for which it was intended.

*An exhibition hall at the De Young Museum in San Francisco, where an attractive corner planting of large Dracaena warneckei, Philodendron selloum, Monstera deliciosa, and Rhapis palms frame an unobtrusive marble bench where the visitor may rest and contemplate a French sculpture of the goddess 'Pomona'. Mellow sunshine diffused through a glass ceiling, and supplementary incandescent spotlights both accent and benefit these showy foliage plants with warm light.*

## Leading Types of Proven House and Decorator Plants

There are thousands of potential subjects in tropical and subtropical plants that may be adaptable for growing indoors. While some very fancy exotics will do well only in a humid conservatory or a glass-enclosed terrarium, a great many species have been introduced in recent years that have been tested for their endurance under adverse conditions of dry steam heat and low light intensity. Limited space permits mention only of a selection of the most satisfactory, easy to maintain and widely favored types. Excellent descriptive and well illustrated books are available which cover this subject exhaustively, including the author's larger EXOTIC PLANT MANUAL (4200 illustrations with expansive text) and the giant EXOTICA, a Pictorial Cyclopedia of Exotic Plants from Tropic and Subtropic Regions (12,000 illustrations on 1834 pg.).

## Plants for Festive Occasions

Flowering plants are joyful envoys of nature to brighten your home, and particularly so during the drab days of winter. To "say it with flowers" is not an empty phrase; flowers tender like no other gift, the deepest sentiments of romance and feelings of good will that we as friends or neighbors

are capable of expressing. There are countless occasions in our lives where we would like to convey to someone our innermost feelings, and never once would the gift of a flowering plant, because of their intrinsic value, be weighed in monetary terms whether lowly and demure, or costly and magnificent. Through flowers we can speak of admiration and of love, of gladness and of heartfelt sympathy, or extend congratulations and best wishes, or merely express good will.

*An "Easter basket" breathing spring, and gay with pastel colors of seasonable potted plants: fragrant Easter-lilies; showy heads of sky-blue Hydrangeas; salmon-pink Azalea 'Coral Bells' and red 'Hexe'; and a deep salmon Polyantha Rose 'Margo Koster'.*

14

"Easter lily",
Lilium longiflorum 'Croft',
a herald of fragrant spring

"Gloxinia"
Sinningia speciosa 'Emperor Frederick'
in season spring and summer

"Dwarf Azalea indica",
Azalea simsii 'Hexe', a compact, free-flowering
tender variety for spring.

"Hortensia", or "Snowballs":
Hydrangea macrophylla 'Merveille',
a showy Easter and Mothers Day plant.

Florists "Mum plant":
Chrysanthemum morifolium 'Yellow Delaware';
normally blooms early November

"Poinsettia" or "Christmas star":
Euphorbia pulcherrima 'Barbara Ecke Supreme',
its starry bracts a holiday symbol

*The noble Orangerie of Louis XIV at Versailles, built in 1681 for the wintering of 1500 citrus trees and palms of the Royal gardens – a forerunner of the Victorian wintergarden.*

# A History of Exotic Indoor Plants

The cultivation of imported and unusual plants has been undertaken since very early times. Through their carvings in stone, we know of plants grown in containers by the ancient empires of Babylon and Egypt. 3,500 years ago, and in China, ornamental horticulture dates back 2,500 years to Confucius and Laotse. The scrolls of Virgil, Horace and Seneca sufficiently prove that among the nations of antiquity, a very strong attachment existed to cultivating strange plants and fruit.

Early in the 15th century, the wealthy merchants of Venice, Florence and Genoa began to introduce the plants of the East into Europe. The Dutch imported species from the East Indies since 1511, and later from South Africa. About the middle of the 16th century a taste for exotic flowering plants and trees began to prevail in France and England amongst the aristocracy. Orangeries and conservatories were erected in increasing numbers in the 17th century. During the early part of the 18th century upwards of 5000 species were introduced in Europe. But the greatest botanical era was from later in the 18th century to the beginning of the 19th, when plants from India, the Americas, Africa and Australia were collected and taken into cultivation with loving skill and care.

The growing of ever-increasing assortments was put on a commercial scale by famous-name nurseries and thus became available to larger numbers of plant-lovers, which resulted in the wide popularity of house plants in Europe today. From the mid-19th century the habit spread to North America where great conservatories on private estates vied with each other to have the most interesting "winter gardens."

Catalogs of early greenhouse ranges such as Pitcher & Manda, Robert Craig, Henry Dreer, Bobbink and Atkins, and Julius Roehrs listed collections of "stove plants" rivalling those of Europe. The Julius Roehrs Company in those early years brought whole shiploads of decorative plants and palms, dormant flowering plants and bulbs across the Atlantic, and had their own collectors of orchids in South America and Southeast Asia for their "Exotic Nurseries."

Today the large conservatories of pioneer millionaires with their skilled gardeners have largely disappeared, but the habit of having living plants about the home, the glassed-in porch or in an attached little greenhouse, has taken hold. There has developed wide interest on the part of many people for living plants in containers, for decoration and livability in homes and apartments; as well as the wide-spread use of ornamental foliage plants in office buildings, museums, professional offices and all modern structures. According to a recent professional survey it was found that there are an average of six or more potted plants in every home. The vogue of using and caring for plants both out of doors and indoors has added greatly to the enrichment of American living. What could be more rewarding and pleasurable than to live with these wonderfully made creations of nature, and to know their origin brings us close to their exotic homelands and a better understanding of their needs.

# Introduction to the Best in Indoor Plants

## Popular Blooming Plants for every season

As the year advances, certain blooming plants have become associated with sentimental or religious holidays as symbolic of the season. We look for the first primroses and azaleas as the heralds of spring, we must have hyacinths and tulips, lilies and hydrangeas to decorate our homes and churches for the Easter season; roses, gloxinias and gardenias follow up to Mother's Day; geraniums and spring bedding plants on the windowsill lead into summer; in the fall what could be more natural than chrysanthemums in their autumn shades, and cyclamen, begonias and fruited plants take over with winter; and a Christmas without poinsettias is now almost unthinkable.

**FLOWERING PLANTS INDOORS**—Holiday blooming plants in pots require much more water and strong light to keep in good condition, than the average foliage plant. We Americans like nice warm homes but unfortunately our popular flowering plants don't like our comfortable temperatures; for long life and extended bloom our rooms are much too warm unless wanted for temporary display. Most holiday plants keep better around 15°C (60°F) during day and 10°C (50°F) at night. Find a location by the window where it is sunny and yet cooler, at least at night, or on the sunporch; also keep away from heating units.

Azaleas, cyclamen, primulas, chrysanthemums, cinerarias, hydrangeas, Christmas cherries, kalanchoe, pyracantha, heathers, lilies, hyacinths, tulips, daffodils, daisies, geraniums, roses, fuchsias, calceolarias, astilbe, begonias all keep better, and for a reasonably long time, at cooler temperatures, and unfold their buds in a normal manner. There is no harm in using them where needed temporarily for display on a table or other piece of furniture, but real dividends are earned if these plants are carried back to a sunny window and a nice cool place for the night. On the other hand, saintpaulia, gloxinias, poinsettias and gardenias should not be exposed to temperatures much below 18°C (65°F) as their flowers and buds, as well as leaves are sensitive to cold and may be severely checked. But stuffy heat is resented by all flowering plants, and with drafts and drying out, is the cause of most complaints.

Most **FLOWERING POTTED PLANTS** seen at holiday times are not easy as subjects for indoor cultivation. The high light intensities required, the amount of watering, and the needed day-night differences in temperature are not usually available in the home; a greenhouse would offer a better chance of success. But there are exceptions, and the most successfully adapted as a house plant is the "African Violet," SAINTPAULIA. There are literally thousands of named varieties, in colors from violet-blue through rose to white, in single and in double-flowered forms. Old-fashioned window-bloomers are ABUTILON, the "Parlor maples", with bell-like flowers resembling Chinese lanterns. IMPATIENS or "Busy-Lizzie" are watery-succulent herbs producing a never-ending succession of spurred flowers in gay colors. HIBISCUS, the "Rose-mallows" have short-lived giant blossoms in brilliant colors but new buds stand by one day after sunny day.

Geraniums, botanically PELARGONIUM, have always been one of our best-loved flowering plants in the sunny window, with attractive foliage usually zoned and often variegated, producing flower clusters in bright colors to chaste white. Some species are grown for their aromatically scented leaves imitating herbs or fruit.

## Bulbous and Tuberous Flowering Plants

When we think of bulbs, it is our garden varieties that first come to mind, such as tulips, hyacinths, narcissus and lilies. These are customarily forced to bloom as joyful heralds of spring. But it is the subtropic and tropic kind of bulbs, corms and tubers that best adapt themselves as companions around the house, perhaps on the window sill during winter, and on the patio in summer, where they may want to take a rest. Best known of these are HIPPEASTRUM, better known as "Amaryllis"; CLIVIA, the "Kafir-lily"; HAEMANTHUS or "Blood flower"; NEOMARICA, the "Apostle plant"; VELTHEIMIA, a "Forest lily"; ZANTEDESCHIA, the "Calla-lilies". Others are LACHENALIAS, HYMENOCALLIS, and IXIA; also ACHIMENES and various SINNINGIAS.

## Garden Plants for the Window

While we think of **BEDDING PLANTS** as subjects to beautify the summer garden, it is fun and a source of pride to grow them in the open window. Nothing will be as profuse with gaily-colored bloom all summer long as a selection of bright Geraniums, in scarlet or pink; sun-loving, multi-colored Petunias, Lantanas, Phlox, Wax begonias, or Fuchsia. We cannot help but think nostalgically of the charming window boxes spilling over with gay color, and so popular in all Alpine countries.

*In your living room, forced Narcissus x poetaz 'Geranium', a "Cluster narcissus", its clay pot dressed in foil to hold moisture—heralds spring with sweet fragrance and cheerful color while a blanket of snow may still be covering the bulbs waiting outdoors.*

17

An assortment of bromeliads will live in a minimum of root-space, as here planted into a ceramic log (l. to r.: Cryptanthus bivittatus minor, Billbergia nutans, Vriesea splendens, Cryptanthus zonatus zebrinus).

Authentic Mexican baking dish of red Jalisco clay, handpainted and glazed—the fireproof kitchenware of the villagers; planted with Euphorbia lactea and E. grandicornis, Aloe arborescens, Agave sisalina, Golden barrel, and Rainbow cactus.

### Begonias for decorative foliage and flower

**BEGONIAS** with their oblique, often very decorative leaves, are old favorites in collections of plant lovers, but with few exceptions require more humidity and fresh air than the modern home provides. B. metallica and its olive-green, silver-haired foliage; B. masoniana with beautiful nile-green, puckered leaves patterned brown; B. serratipetala with small angelwinged foliage spotted pink, are examples of somewhat more resistant types. Double-flowered varieties of B. semper-florens, the "Rose begonia", are endearing small bloomers for the window sill.

### Bromeliads, the Pineapple family

**BROMELIADS** or "Natural vase plants" are a family peculiar to the Western hemisphere, a distinguished group of plants dwelling as epiphytes on trees and rocks, or as terrestrials on the forest floor, and to which belong some of our most fascinating and decorative ornamentals. They usually form rosettes of leathery, concave leaves, many with bizarre design or strikingly variegated. Their flowers may be hidden deep in the center surrounded by a cup of brilliant crimson inner leaves as in NEOREGELIAS and NIDULARIUM. AECHMEAS and GUZMANIAS form colorful spikes or heads of long-lasting leathery bracts or bright berries. BILLBERGIAS are tubular in shape and their showy inflorescence with blue flowers inclines to be pendant. Most TILLANDSIAS and VRIESEAS have spear-like flattened, colorful flower spikes. The terrestrial CRYPTANTHUS, the "Earth stars", are more or less flattened rosettes with striking leaf design mottled, striped or tiger-banded in silver over greens and bronzes.

### Gesneriads, the African Violet family

This giant family includes hundreds of handsome, often velvety-leaved plants with showy wheel-shaped, tubular, or bell-like flowers.

The Western hemisphere offers the greatest wealth in species of **GESNERIADS** in cultivation today. Most important of this tropical American group are the SINNINGIAS, better known as "Gloxinias"; then COLUMNEAS with their brilliant flowers; EPISCIAS with carpeted leaves; ACHIMENES, the "Magic flower"; SMITHIANTHA, the "Temple bells"; KOHLERIAS looking like little gloxinia trees; and RECHSTEINERIAS which include the scarlet "Cardinal flowers", and the silver-hairy "Brazilian Edelweiss". Many curious gesneriads come from Asia.

Africa is not so rich on species, but from a rather small area in East Africa originate the various SAINTPAULIA, which as the "African violet" is easily today the most admired little flowering plant in the American home. Endemic in Africa also is STREPTOCARPUS, the "Cape primrose".

### Orchid-family — Queen of Exotics

The aristocratic **ORCHID FAMILY** presents a more difficult and rather specialized subject for successful home cultivation, usually due to lack of light, uncontrollable temperature, and insufficient ventilation with humidity. There are some genera that promise good flowering results to the average indoor gardener: the epiphytic EPIDENDRUM, a very willing bloomer with waxy, usually fragrant, often greenish blossoms; a good example is E. cochleatum, the "Cockle-shelled orchid". Another satisfactory group are the ONCIDIUM, or "Butterfly orchids", with brightly colored, long-lasting yellow flowers marked brown, often in large sprays; recommended for home culture are O. flexuo-sum, the "Dancing dolls" and O. spathelatum, the "Golden shower".

18

## Fancy Flowering Plants and Shrubs

**FLOWERING PLANTS** for pots or tubs could easily separate into two groups: the kind we popularly associate with holiday giving and produced and timed by commercial growers as seasonal blooming plants; and another category, less common but of a type that can be grown as a hobby and cared for at home. To bring these into flower may present a challenge but would bring a wonderful feeling of satisfaction and sense of pride to a real plant lover.

**SHRUBBY PLANTS** usually, with some exception, prefer an intermediate or even cooler temperature at night, and enjoy being set outdoors for the summer.

## Fruited and Berried plants in containers

There has always been a strong desire to produce **EDIBLE FRUIT** on a windowsill. If light and ventilation are good, success may be had with the "Calamondin orange" CITRUS mitis, C. 'Meyeri', the "Dwarf Chinese lemon", and C. 'Ponderosa', the "American wonder lemon". The "Figtree", FICUS carica will also yield edible fruit if space permits, so would the "Chinese dwarf banana", MUSA nana; and the "Dwarf pomegranate", PUNICA granatum nana. ANANAS comosus, the "Pineapple", cultivated in a pot, also brings forth its golden fruit, and the "Coffee tree", COFFEA arabica, with sufficient age and light will bear not only sweetly fragrant flowers, but also its juicy crimson berries each containing a pair of coffee beans.

## Glamorous exotic Foliage plants

There are many **BROAD-LEAVED WOODY EVERGREENS** that have found a place in indoor decorative schemes. BRASSAIA actinophylla, the "Queensland umbrella tree", better known as Schefflera, has become an ideal house and decorator plant. With spreading crowns of palmately divided, glossy green leaves, it ideally fills a corner, though keeping best in a light and warm location. Another picturesque araliad is POLYSCIAS fruticosa, the "Ming aralia", with willowy, twisting stems densely clothed toward their tops with fern-like, lacy foliage.

The so-called "Rubber trees" of the varied genus FICUS are widely used in homes and offices. All require good light to hold their foliage well. Best known are the large-leaved F. elastica 'Decora', but perhaps even more attractive because of their very graceful habit are several small-leaved kinds, such as F. benjamina, retusa and nitida. The giant violin-like, leathery leaves of F. lyrata, better known as pandurata, are a most magnificent attraction in an indoor foliage tree. COCCOLOBA, the "Sea grape" is another sturdy, woody plant, somewhat resembling Ficus, with leathery, rounded leaves and crimson veining.

**DRACAENAS,** the "Dragon trees" are good house plant subjects. D. marginata from Madagascar forms clusters of flexuous, artistically twisted stems topped by terminal rosettes of narrow, leathery leaves of great appeal to decorators. D. deremensis 'Warneckei' is a handsome, symmetrical rosette of sword-shaped, milky-green leaves striped white. D. sanderiana, the "Ribbon plant", is a diminutive and slender, highly variegated species, which may also be grown in water-culture.

Not related but similar in appearance is the old favorite PANDANUS veitchii, a "Screwpine", a rosette of leathery sword-shaped leaves arranged in spirals, glossy green attractively banded white.

*Delicate Gesneriads, mainly Episcias, are good subjects for culture under fluorescent light in the home, at the same time high-lighting the colorful patterns of their carpet-like foliage.*

*Philodendron selloum growing above Iguassu Falls, in Western Brazil*

## Aroids — the indispensable House plant family

In the **AROID FAMILY,** which has given us many good "long life" houseplants, most prominent are several <u>PHILODENDRON</u>. These are handsome tropical American mostly scandent plants with <u>attractive leathery foliage, heart-shaped, slashed, to skeleton-shaped; most are</u> <u>excellent keepers and eventually need some support.</u> MONSTERA deliciosa, often known as Philodendron pertusum, the "Swiss-cheese plant" has showy glossy, perforated leaves slashed to the margins.

<u>DIEFFENBACHIA</u>, the "Dumbcanes", in a number of attractive species, are handsome tropical American foliage plants usually with <u>beautifully variegated leaves; they tolerate much neglect and</u> <u>thrive even in a dry living room.</u> AGLAONEMA, the "Chinese evergreens", are <u>smallish tropical</u> <u>Asiatic, fleshy herbs of slow growth, with leathery leaves often painted with silvery or colorful pat-</u> <u>terns; very durable and tolerant.</u>

<u>SCINDAPSUS,</u> popularly known as Pothos, the "Ivy-arums", are tropical climbers from the Malaysian monsoon area, with usually <u>attractive variegated leaves small in the juvenile stage.</u> They luxuriate in warm, even super-heated atmosphere.

SPATHIPHYLLUM, the "Peace lilies"; easy-growing, <u>vigorous tropical herbs</u> forming clumps, with happy-green foliage, and a succession of flower-like inflorescence resembling Anthurium, usually white. <u>ANTHURIUMS themselves, with their colorful spathes,</u> such as the "Flamingo flower", are <u>rather difficult to maintain without humid greenhouse or terrarium.</u>

<u>CALADIUMS</u> are tropical American tuberous herbs producing <u>fragile-looking but gorgeously</u> <u>colorful foliage in a rainbow of colors, that will keep surprisingly well if protected from chills and</u> <u>wintry drafts.</u>

## Palms and palm-like plants for Interiors

Because of their majestic beauty and distinctive decorative appeal there is no limit to the number of types of palms that lend themselves to indoor use. Best known of feather palms is the "Paradise palm", HOWEIA, better known as Kentia. This long-suffering, noble species combines natural grace with sturdiness, and its thick-leathery leaves will stand much abuse. Lately, the charming "Parlor palms", and "Bamboo palms" of the genus CHAMAEDOREA have come into vogue; their dainty fronds on slender stalks keep well even in places fairly dark. Similar in appearance is the "Areca palm", CHRYSALIDOCARPUS, growing in dense clusters, with slender yellowish stems carrying feathery pinnate fronds. The "Pygmy date", PHOENIX roebelenii, a trunk-forming, compact plant with gracefully arching, dark green leaves is an excellent houseplant if kept warm and moist.

## Conifers for containers, and dwarfed Bonsai

**CONIFEROUS EVERGREENS** generally <u>prefer the cooler regions outdoors.</u> But from along the subtropical zone comes ARAUCARIA heterophylla, better known as excelsa, the "<u>Norfolk</u> <u>Island pine", an undemanding graceful conifer</u> with formal tiered branches of fresh green needles, <u>long-lived even in dark corners, in any temperature short of freezing.</u> PODOCARPUS, the somber "Buddhist pine" forms dense pyramids of dark green needle-like leaves; <u>prefers cooler locations.</u>

**ART OF BONSAI:** Shaped Bonsai, or dwarfed trees, grown in shallow earthenware containers, are objects of loving care and admiration in every home in Japan. Though this cult had evolved out of China early in the 12th century, yet here in America it is as new as tomorrow. The ultimate aim of the subtle art of Bonsai is to control the growth of a normal plant by constant and skillful pruning and shaping to attain the stately shape of ancient big trees in miniature. The trunk of the tree, the spread of the roots, the distribution of branches are all used to give an aged appearance to the tree. The Japanese white pine, Pinus parviflora, is widely used in Japan as an apt subject for bonsai work. Other pines can similarly be used.

## Ferns and Fern-allies

**FERNS** come in a wide variety of forms, gracefully bold in huge palm-like treeferns, to daintily petite from the humid forest floor, in close to 12,000 species. One of the best of treeferns are the Hawaiian CIBOTIUM, of great appeal to decorators. Their stout, fibrous trunk bears a crown of magnificent, light green fronds. Best-known of smaller Parlor ferns is the ubiquitous "Sword fern", NEPHROLEPIS; bushy rosettes in variable forms from plain pinnate fronds in the "Boston fern" to very feathery. Another old-fashioned friend is the "Holly-fern" CYRTOMIUM, with glossy-dark leaves as tough as leather. Also leathery but lacy is the "Leather fern" RUMOHRA. The "Birdsnest fern", ASPLENIUM nidus, forms a rosette of parchment-textured, fan-like, light green leaves. POLYPODIUMS are often known as "Hare's-foot fern" because of their paw-like woolly rhizomes, their feathery leaves on slender stalks are quite long-lasting. The DAVALLIAS or "Rabbit's-foot ferns" likewise have slender creeping, furry rhizomes which bear on wiry stalks their finely lacy but leathery fronds. Amongst our best-loved ferns are the dainty "Maiden-hairs", ADIANTUM in several species. However, these need high humidity for best success. The so-called "Table ferns" are a varied group of mainly PTERIS and PELLAEA. Some are frilly, others variegated, and in their small stage are ideal for terrariums. PLATYCERIUM, or "Staghorn ferns" always have aroused the greatest curiosity because of their weird shapes. Growing as epiphytes on trees, their sterile fronds cling snugly to the bark of trees, or in cultivation a wire basket or wooden block, while their much-divided fertile leaves resemble the antlers of deer or elk.

There are popular **FERN-LIKE PLANTS** such as ASPARAGUS, simple house plants with plumy fronds much used for cut. The pretty SELAGINELLAS, ominously called "Sweat plants" or "Moss ferns" are strictly warm terrarium subjects, as their delicate fronds greedily soak up moisture from the atmosphere to keep from shrivelling.

## Glamorous exotic Foliage plants

We know a great many charming, smallish **FOLIAGE PLANTS** from the tropical forest floor, often with strikingly patterned foliage, some of which have become remarkably good houseplants. Amongst them are several MARANTAS, the "Prayer plants", folding their attractive leaves at night, and the exquisite CALATHEA makoyana, the "Peacockplant", with translucent foliage beautifully painted with a feathery peacock design. PILEA cadierei, the silvery "Aluminum plant" is a willing grower with fleshy leaves splashed silver. "Crotons", botanically CODIAEUM, are magnificent, multicolored foliage plants, but need maximum light and warmth to hold their foliage and coloration well. Although primarily thought of as bedding plants, the vari-colored COLEUS, or "Painted nettles", are gorgeous herbaceous foliage plants that will decorate a sunny window with a brilliant array of color.

There are many different, charming little "Pepperfaces" of the genus PEPEROMIA. Forming miniature rosettes or slowly vining, their waxy foliage is variously attractive, corrugated, painted with silver, or highly variegated with creamy-white.

*Charming attractions: Pilea cadierei, the silvery "Aluminum plant" or "Watermelon pilea" (left), and Geogenanthus undatus, the "Seersucker plant" with quilted leaves (right).*

## Shamrock and Oxalis

The characteristic trifoliate leaves so typical of the true clover, or Trifolium, belonging to the Leguminosae family, are common also within the genus Oxalis of the Oxalidaceae, and for this reason both these are popularly known as "Shamrock", adapted from the Irish word for clover. Since both Trifolium and Oxalis are present in Ireland there is no certainty as to the exact identity of which of these Shamrocks was picked by St. Patrick as the symbol of Trinity.

**OXALIS AS HOUSE PLANTS**—In the Oxalis there are many wonderful little house plants for the sunny window, their pretty flowers of white, yellow, pink or rosy-red blooming tirelessly, opening only to the sun. The tender Oxalis in cultivation are primarily from the Andes of Chile and Peru to Brazil and north to Mexico, and are well represented in South Africa.

## Vines and Basket plants

**VINES AND TRAILERS** are actually weeping plants with stems too weak to support themselves, and occur in almost all plant families, in an endless variety of character and form. Best known are many variations of "Ivy" in the genus HEDERA. Generally they prefer a cool location, but some small-leaved or variegated varieties will do quite well on the window-sill. Several CISSUS such as C. rhombifolia, the "Grape ivy" with metallic foliage, and the leathery C. antarctica or "Kangaroo ivy" are recommended for planter boxes or room dividers. Intriguing are the slow-growing HOYAS, or "Waxvines", with leathery foliage and waxy, wheel-shaped blooms. By contrast, the "Inch plants" and "Wandering Jews", TRADESCANTIA and ZEBRINA, are rapid growers with watery stems and vari-colored leaves—long-beloved old houseplants for window-shelf or hanging baskets. The "Purple passion vine", GYNURA 'Sarmentosa', is entirely covered with purple, bristly hairs.

The "Spiderplants" of the genus CHLOROPHYTUM, long known as Anthericum, are modest house plant favorites, forming clustering rosettes of fresh green ribbon leaves banded white; young plantlets develop from arching stalks—ideal in hanging pots.

There are many tropical scandent clamberers with beautiful flowers, such as PASSIFLORA, ALLAMANDA, JASMINUM and CLERODENDRUM, but in windows of insufficient size and in the absence of strong light they hesitate to bloom.

## Succulents, including Cacti, for easy care

**CACTI** are native to the Western hemisphere, frugal plants that have developed a special capacity to store water in thick, fleshy bodies. They are children of the sun and love light. Needing a minimum of care and very little water, many species have become popular house plants on a sunny window sill.

With some 2000 species, there are a great many, often curious forms, from the tiny "Pincushions", MAMMILLARIAS; PARODIA or "Tom Thumb" cactus, and REBUTIA, the "Pigmy cactus", both of which willingly bloom when young and tiny; GYMNOCALYCIUM or "Chin cactus"; NOTOCACTUS or "Ball cactus"; to the ECHINOCACTUS or "Barrel"; various OPUNTIAS, the "Bunny ears" and "Chollas"; CEPHALOCEREUS or "Old man" with its glistening white hair. Of larger habit the column types of CEREUS and its relatives, often night-blooming, to giant landmarks of the desert such as CARNEGIEA, the "Saguaro", with branching columns reaching 15 meters (50 ft.). Dwellers of tropical forests are many epiphytic RHIPSALIS, the "Mistletoe", or the near epiphytic "Orchid cacti", EPIPHYLLUM, with their magnificent blooms in shimmering shades of color, suitable for growing in baskets.

Other **SUCCULENTS** abound in arid regions of the world, and these also have become favorite subjects for the window sill, or arranged in glazed pottery as dishgardens on desk or table. Belonging to many unrelated families, succulents have in common fleshy stems or leaves capable of storing water. Typical stem-succulents are the EUPHORBIAS, with their often angled candelabra columns resembling cacti. Leaf succulents are represented by ALOE, famous since ancient times as the "Medicine plants"; ECHEVERIAS or "Hen-and-chicks", KALANCHOE tomentosa, the silvery "Panda plant"; CRASSULAS as in the "Jade plant", and HAWORTHIAS, rosettes with pearly-dotted leaves. Quite durable pot plants are the frugal strap-leaf "Snake plants" or SANSEVIERIAS, and they are often seen in unfavorable locations tolerating much neglect.

*Glazed ceramic planter featuring the heart-warming Disney fawn "Bambi", as planted with an assortment of miniature succulent plants such as kalanchoe, sedum, crassula and aloe. This modest arrangement enhances a corner of the living room, requiring a minimum of attention.*

Begonia x hiemalis (elatior)
'Rieger's Schwabenland'

Cyclamen persicum 'Perle von Zehlendorf',
"Florists cyclamen" or "Alpine violet"
winter-flowering vivid salmon, for cool locations

Erica gracilis, the "Rose heath"
covered with tiny rosy bells from autumn on

Kalanchoe blossfeldiana 'Tom Thumb'
a dwarf, very compact "Flaming Katy"
with masses of red flowers in late winter

Calceolaria herbeohybrida 'Multiflora nana',
"Lady's pocketbook", a cool spring plant

Senecio cruentus 'Multiflora nana',
small-flowered "Cineraria" of florists

Hydrangea macr. 'Strafford'
clear rosy-red, firm

Rosa x grandiflora
'Queen Elizabeth'
free flowering soft rose-pink

Rosa x polyantha 'Mothers-day'
deep crimson "Baby rose"

Begonia x hiemalis 'Apricot Beauty'
*"Apricot winter begonia", best where cool*

Begonia x cheimantha 'Lady Mac'
*"Christmas begonia" or "Busy Lizzie begonia"*

Fuchsia x hybrida 'Winston Churchill'
"Lady's eardrops"; red sepals, blue skirt

Begonia semperflorens 'Pink Pearl'
shapely 'Wax begonia", rich pink

Petunia x hybrida 'California Giant'
showy "Giant pot petunia"

Lantana camara
"Shrub verbena", yellow to orange

Gardenia jasminoides 'Veitchii',
fragrant "Everblooming gardenia"

Astilbe japonica 'Gladstone',
perennial "Spiraea" forced for Easter

Chrysanthemum morifolium 'Golden Lace'
"Spider mum" or "Fuji" type

Chrysanthemum morifolium 'Princess Ann'
excellent "Pot mum", of the "decorative" class

Primula obconica
"German primrose", for winter-spring

Begonia semperflorens fl. pl. 'Lady Frances'
everblooming "Rose begonia" with coppery foliage

Chrysanthemum frutescens
"White Marguerite" or "Paris daisy"

Pelargonium x domesticum
'Earliana'
*a bushy, free-blooming "Pansy geranium"*

**Tulipa 'Makassar'**
yellow Triumph tulip

**Tulipa 'Kees Nelis'**
Triumph tulip red, edged yellow

**Hyacinthus 'Pink Pearl'**
rose pink Dutch hyacinth

Convallaria majalis, a perennial,
forced "Lily-of-the-Valley", sweetly fragrant

Muscari armeniacum 'Heavenly Blue',
spring-blooming "Grape hyacinth"

**Crocus 'Vernus hybrid'**
*"Alpine spring crocus"*

**Crinum x powellii**
*"Powell's swamp lily"*

**Ixia x 'Rose Queen'**
*"Rosy corn-lily"*

**Zantedeschia elliottiana**
*"Yellow calla" of hort.*

**Zantedeschia aethiopica**
*"White calla-lily"*

**Hymenocallis narcissiflora**
(Ismene calathina)
*"Basket flower"*

**Eucharis grandiflora**
*"Amazon lily"*

**Haemanthus katherinae**
*"Blood flower"*

**Clivia miniata 'Grandiflora'**
*"Scarlet kafir lily"*

**Scilla peruviana**
*"Cuban lily" from Madeira*

**Polianthes tuberosa**
*sweetly scented "Tuberose"*

**Neomarica northiana**
*"Walking iris"*

**Hippeastrum vittatum**
*"Striped amaryllis"*

**Hippeastrum (leopoldii) 'Claret'**
*crimson "Dutch amaryllis"*

**Amaryllis belladonna**
*the "Cape belladonna"*

**Hippeastrum striatum fulgidum**
*"Everblooming amaryllis"*

**Veltheimia viridifolia**
*"Forest-lily"*

**Lachenalia lilacina**
*"Lavender Cape cowslip"*

**Urginea maritima, the "Sea onion"**

**Ornithogalum caudatum**
*"False sea-onion"· or "Healing onion"*

**Agapanthus africanus**
*"Blue African lily"*

Senecio cineraria 'Diamond'
"*Dusty miller*"

Coleus blumei 'Defiance'
"*Painted nettle*"

Impatiens hawkeri 'Exotica'
from New Guinea

Iresine herbstii
'Aureo-reticulata'
"*Chicken-gizzard*"

Impatiens oliveri
"*Giant touch-me-not*"

Phlox drummondii
"*Dwarf annual phlox*"

Impatiens walleriana var.
sultanii 'Variegata'
"*Variegated patient Lucy*"

Impatiens platypetala aurantiaca
"*Tangerine impatiens*"

Impatiens walleriana var. holstii
"*Busy Lizzie*"

Pelargonium x hortorum 'Pygmy',
*miniature, vivid red*

Pelargonium x hortorum 'Antares',
*burning dark scarlet*

Pelargonium x hortorum 'Irene'
popular pot geranium

Pelargonium peltatum
*"Ivy geranium"*

Pelargonium peltatum 'L'Elegante'
*"Sunset ivy geranium"*

Pelargonium x hortorum
'Miss Burdett Coutts'
*beautiful "Tricolor geranium"*

Fuchsia triphylla
'Gartenmeister Bohnstedt'
*"Honeysuckle fuchsia"*

Catharanthus roseus
(Vinca rosea in hort.)
*"Madagascar periwinkle"*

Pelargonium x hortorum
'Wilhelm Langguth'
*flowers cherry red*

Pelargonium x limoneum ("Lemon geranium")
P. 'Prince Rupert' (lemon-scented)
P. 'Prince Rupert variegated'

P. grossularioides hort. ("Gooseberry")
P. graveolens 'Minor' ("Little-leaf rose")
P. 'Torento' ("Ginger geranium")

P. graveolens ("Rose geranium")
P. capitatum 'Attar of Roses'
P. graveolens 'Variegatum' ("Mint-scented rose")

P. x fragrans ("Nutmeg geranium")
P. denticulatum ("Pine geranium")
P. dent. filicifolium ("Fernleaf geranium")

P. 'M. Ninon' ("Apricot geranium")
P. tomentosum ("Peppermint geranium")
P. quercifolium 'Fair Ellen' ("Oakleaf ger.")

P. x nervosum ("Lime geranium")
P. 'Prince of Orange' ("Orange geranium")
P. odoratissimum ("Apple geranium")

Begonia serratipetala
*"Pink spot angelwing"*

Begonia x'Corallina de Lucerna'

Begonia x argenteo-guttata
*"Trout-begonia"*

Begonia coccinea
*"Angelwing begonia"*

Begonia 'Sachsen'

Begonia 'Pink Parade'

Begonia hispida cucullifera
*"Piggyback begonia"*

Begonia scharffii (haageana)
*"Elephant-ear begonia"*

Begonia x'Viaudii'

Begonia schmidtiana

Begonia hydrocotylifolia
*"Miniature pond-lily"*

Begonia bartonea
*"Winter jewel"*

Begonia fernandoi-costa

Begonia sceptrum (aconitifolia 'Hild. Schneider')

Begonia x margaritacea

Begonia eminii (mannii)
*"Roseleaf begonia"*

Begonia egregia (quadrilocularis)

Begonia x'Veitch's Carmine'

Begonia boweri
*"Miniature eyelash begonia"*

Begonia semp. albo-foliis 'Maine Variety'
*"Calla-lily begonia"*

Begonia x'Alto-Scharff'

Begonia scharffiana

Begonia scabrida

Begonia bradei

Begonia leptotricha
"*Woolly bear*"

Begonia x'Braemar'

Begonia venosa

Begonia kellermannii

Begonia incana

Begonia x'Thurstonii'

**Begonia metallica**
*"Metallic-leaf begonia"*

Begonia x margaritae

Begonia x credneri

**Begonia vitifolia**
*"Grapeleaf begonia"*

Begonia 'Nelly Bly'

Begonia epipsila

**Begonia ulmifolia**
*"Elm-leaf begonia"*

Begonia involucrata

Begonia x erythrophylla 'Bunchii'
*"Curly kidney begonia"*

Begonia manicata
'Aureo-maculata crispa'

Begonia x erythrophylla helix
*"Whirlpool begonia"*

Begonia x fuscomaculata

Begonia x ricinifolia
*"Bronze leaf begonia"*

Begonia heracleifolia nigricans

Begonia 'Immense'

Begonia heracleifolia
*"Star begonia", "Parsnip begonia"*

Begonia goegoensis
*"Fire king begonia"*

Begonia masoniana
*"Iron cross begonia"*

Begonia versicolor
*"Fairy carpet begonia"*

Begonia pustulata
*"Blister begonia"*

Begonia imperialis
*"Carpet begonia"*

Begonia x'Cleopatra'
*"Mapleleaf begonia"*

Begonia rex 'Merry Christmas'

Begonia rex 'Helen Teupel'
*"Diadema hybrid"*

Begonia rex 'President' ('Pres. Carnot')

Begonia rex 'Comtesse Louise Erdoedy'
*"Corkscrew begonia"*

Begonia x'Elsie M. Frey'

Begonia limmingheiana (glaucophylla)
*"Shrimp begonia"*

Aechmea caudata variegata
"Billbergia forgetii" hort.

Aechmea chantinii
*"Amazonian zebra plant"*

Ananas bracteatus 'Striatus'
*"Variegated wild pineapple"*

Ananas comosus variegatus
*"Variegated pineapple"*

Aechmea x 'Royal Wine'

Aechmea fasciata
*"Silver vase"*

Aechmea weilbachii leodiensis
*"Tropical lilac"*

Aechmea miniata discolor
*"Purplish Coral-berry"*

Aechmea fulgens
*"Coral berry"*

Aechmea mariae-reginae
*"Queen aechmea"*

Quesnelia marmorata
*"Grecian vase"*

Aechmea x 'Fosters Favorite'
*"Lacquered wine-cup"*

Aechmea x'Bert'

**Billbergia x 'Fantasia'**
*"Marbled rainbow plant"*

**Billbergia pyramidalis concolor**
*"Summer torch"*

**Billbergia nutans**
*"Queen's tears", "Indoor oats"*

**Billbergia macrocalyx**
*"Fluted urn"*

**Billbergia saundersii**
*"Rainbow plant"*

**Billbergia pyramidalis 'Striata'**
*"Striped urn plant"*

**Billbergia x 'Albertii'**
*"Friendship plant"*

**Billbergia x 'Santa Barbara'**
*"Banded urn plant"*

**Billbergia pyramidalis**
**var. pyramidalis**

Cryptanthus acaulis ruber
*"Miniature red earth star"*

Cryptanthus bivittatus minor
(roseus pictus)
*"Dwarf rose-stripe star"*

Cryptanthus lacerdae
*"Silver star"*

Cryptanthus x rubescens
*"Brown earth star"*

Cryptanthus acaulis
*"Green earth star"*

Cryptanthus x osyanus
*"Mottled earth-star"*

Cryptanthus bivittatus
lueddemannii
*"Large rose-stripe star"*

Dyckia brevifolia
*"Miniature agave"*

Dyckia fosteriana
*"Silver and gold dyckia"*

Cryptanthus zonatus zebrinus
*"Pheasant leaf"*

Cryptanthus diversifolius
*"Vary-leaf star"*

Cryptanthus x 'It'
*"Color-band"*

Cryptanthus beuckeri
*"Marbled spoon"*

Cryptanthus fosterianus
*"Stiff pheasant-leaf"*

Cryptanthus bromelioides tricolor
*"Rainbow star"*

Cryptanthus zonatus
*"Zebra plant"*

**Neoregelia carolinae 'Marechalii'**
*"Blushing bromeliad"*

**Neoregelia carolinae 'Tricolor'**
*"Striped blushing bromeliad"*

**Neoregelia farinosa**
*"Crimson cup"*

**Neoregelia x'Mar-Con'**
**(marmorata x concentrica)**
*"Marbled fingernail"*

**Neoregelia spectabilis**
*"Fingernail plant"*

**Neoregelia mooreana**
*"Ossifragi vase"*

**Neoregelia tristis**
*"Miniature marble plant"*

**Neoreglia x'Marmorata hybrid'**
*"Marbled fingernail plant"*

**Neoregelia sarmentosa chlorosticta**

Vriesea x mariae
*"Painted feather"*

Vriesea splendens 'Major'
*"Flaming sword"*

Vriesea imperialis
*"Giant vriesea"*
in the Organ Mountains, Brazil

Vriesea hieroglyphica
*"King of bromeliads"*

Guzmania lingulata 'Major'
*"Scarlet star"*

Tillandsia lindenii
*"Blue-flowered torch"*

Nidularium innocentii nana
*"Miniature birdsnest"*

Guzmania musaica
*"Mosaic vase"*

Guzmania lingulata 'Minor'
*"Orange star"*

Tillandsia usneoides
*"Spanish moss"*

Tillandsia flexuosa
*"Spiralled airplant"*

Tillandsia fasciculata
*"Wild pine"*

**Achimenes ehrenbergii**
*orchid-colored*

**Achimenes erecta (coccinea)**
*scarlet "Cupid's bower"*

**Achimenes longiflora 'Andersonii'**
*purplish "Trumpet achimenes"*

**Aeschynanthus pulcher**
*"Royal red bugler"*

**Aeschynanthus marmoratus**
*"Zebra basket vine"*

**Alloplectus schlimii**
shimmering light green

**Columnea verecunda**
*bright yellow*

**Columnea microphylla**
*"Small-leaved goldfish vine"*

**Columnea linearis**
*rose pink flowers*

**Episcia reptans (fulgida)**
*blood-red flowers*

**Episcia lilacina 'Lilacina'**
*"Blue-flowered teddy-bear"*

**Episcia cupreata 'Acajou'**
*blooms orange-scarlet*

**Diastema quinquevulnerum**
*white flowers dotted purple*

**Chirita lavandulacea**
*blue "Hindustan gentian"*

**Gloxinia perennis (maculata)**
*"Canterbury bell gloxinia"*

**Kohleria lindeniana**
*vivid green with silver veins*

**Kohleria tubiflora**
*"Painted kohleria"*

**Kohleria 'Eriantha hybrid'**
*known as Isoloma hirsutum*

Streptocarpus x hybridus
*"Hybrid cape primrose", in many colors*

Rechsteineria leucotricha
*"Rainha do Abismo" or "Brazilian edelweiss"*

Gesneria cuneifolia
(Pentarhaphia reticulata)
*"Fire cracker"*

Rechsteineria cardinalis
*"Cardinal flower"*

Sinningia pusilla
*"Miniature slipper plant"*

Sinningia regina
*"Cinderella slippers"*

Sinningia speciosa
*"Violet slipper gloxinia"*

Smithiantha zebrina (Naegelia)
*bells scarlet with yellow*

**Saintpaulia ionantha**
*original "African violet", violet-blue*

**Saintpaulia rupicola**
*"Kenya violet", wisteria-blue*

**Saintpaulia diplotricha**
*pale violet flowers*

**Saintpaulia confusa (kewensis hort.)**
*"Usambara violet", pale blue*

**Saintpaulia 'Star Girl'**
*"Girl-leaf single"*

**S. 'Blue Boy-in-the-Snow'**
*"Leaves mottled cream"*

**Saintpaulia 'Rhapsodie Elfriede'**
*European triploid*

**Saintpaulia 'Kenya Violet'**
*"Long-lasting double violet-blue"*

**Saintpaulia 'Diana'**
*"European single violet"*

Bifrenaria harrisoniae
(Brazil)

Angraecum sesquipedale
*"Star of Bethlehem orchid"*
(Madagascar)

Chysis aurea
(Mexico)

Brassia gireoudiana
*"Spider orchid"*
(Costa Rica)

Brassavola nodosa
*"Lady of the night"*
(Costa Rica)

Brassavola digbyana
(Honduras)

Brassia verrucosa
*"Queen's umbrella"*
(Central America)

Haemaria discolor dawsoniana
*"Golden lace orchid"*
(Malaya)

Aerides crassifolium
*"King of Aerides"*
(Burma)

**Cycnoches egertonianum**
*(Mexico), female flowers*

**Catasetum saccatum christyanum**
(Brazil: Amazon)

**Calanthe x bella**
*East Indian terrestrial*

**Cymbidium 'Flirtation'**
*"Miniature hybrid cymbidium"*

**Cymbidium x alexanderi**
*"Corsage cymbidium"*

**Coelogyne lawrenceana**
(Vietnam)

**Coelogyne sparsa**
(Philippines)

**Coelogyne cristata**
(Nepal Himalayas)

**Coelogyne dayana**
*"Neck-lace orchid"*
(Sumatra)

Cattleya intermedia alba
*a "Cocktail orchid"*
(Brazil)

Cattleya dowiana aurea
*"Queen cattleya"*
(Colombia)

Cattleya mossiae
*"Easter orchid"*
(Venezuela)

Cattleya skinneri
(Guatemala)

Cattleya lueddemanniana
(Brazil)

Cattleya forbesii
*another "Cocktail orchid"*
(Brazil)

Cattleya bowringiana
*a "Cluster cattleya"*
(Honduras)

Cattleya trianaei
*"Christmas orchid"*
(Colombia)

Epidendrum stamfordianum
(Guatemala to Colombia)

Epidendrum brassavolae
(Guatemala)

Epidendrum prismatocarpum
*"Rainbow orchid"*
(Costa Rica)

Epidendrum pentotis
(C. America to Brazil)

Epidendrum mariae
(So. Mexico)

Epidendrum radiatum
(Mexico)

Epidendrum ibaguense (radicans)
*"Fiery reed orchid"*
(Mexico to Peru)

Epidendrum cochleatum
*"Cockle-shelled orchid"*
(W. Indies, C. America)

Epidendrum atropurpureum
*"Spice orchid"*
(Mexico to Brazil)

Dendrobium falconeri
(India)

Dendrobium phalaenopsis
(Queensland, New Guinea)

Dendrobium thyrsiflorum
(Burma)

Dendrobium johnsoniae
(New Guinea)

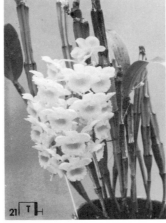

Dendrobium densiflorum
(Himalayas, Burma)

Dendrobium aggregatum
(lindleyii) (Yunnan)

Dendrobium nobile
(Himalayas to Yunnan)

Dendrobium primulinum
(Himalayas, Burma)

Dendrobium moschatum
(Himalayas, Burma)

Laelia purpurata
"Queen of orchids" in So. Brazil

Laelia perrinii
(Brazil)

x Epiphronitis veitchii
(Epidendrum x Sophronitis)

Dendrochilum glumaceum (syn. Platyclinis)
*"Chain orchid"*
(Philippines)

Lycaste deppei
(So. Mexico)

Lycaste virginalis alba
*"White Nun"*
(Guatemala)

Lycaste aromatica
(Mexico)

Oncidium flexuosum
*"Dancing doll orchid"*
(Brazil, Paraguay)

Oncidium splendidum
(Guatemala)

Oncidium sarcodes
(Brazil)

Oncidium stipitatum
(Panama)

Oncidium lanceanum
*"Leopard orchid"*
(Trinidad, Guyana)

Oncidium sphacelatum
*"Golden shower"*
(Mexico to Honduras)

Miltonia roezlii alba
white *"Pansy orchid"*
(Colombia)

Masdevallia veitchiana
(Peru)

Maxillaria picta
(Brazil)

Phalaenopsis amabilis 'Summit Snow'
*glistening white "Moth orchid"*
(Malaya, Indonesia)

Phragmipedium caudatum (syn. Selenipedium)
*"Mandarin orchid"*
(Peru, Ecuador)

Odontoglossum crispum
*"Lace orchid"*
(Colombia)

Odontoglossum grande
*"Tiger orchid"*
(Mexico)

Odontoglossum pulchellum
*"Lily of the valley orchid"*
(Guatemala)

Phaius wallichii
*"Nun orchid"*
(Sikkim)

Vanilla fragrans 'Marginata'
*"Variegated vanilla"*

Schomburgkia undulata
(Trinidad, Venezuela)

Vanda tricolor
*"Tricolor strap vanda"*
(Java)

Vanda coerulea
*"Blue orchid"*
(Himalayas)

Vanda x 'Miss Agnes Joaquim'
*"Hawaiian corsage orchid"*
*"Moon orchid"*

Paph. callosum splendens
(Thailand, Vietnam)

Paphiopedilum x maudiae
*exquisite hybrid, green and white*

Paphiopedilum insigne
*"Lady slipper"*
(Himalayas)

Paphiopedilum rothschildianum
(Papua, Borneo)

Zygopetalum mackayi
(Brazil: Serra do Mar)

Paphiopedilum godefroyae
(Vietnam, Thailand)

**Abutilon megapotamicum variegatum**
*"Weeping Chinese lantern"*

**Abutilon x hybridum**
*"Flowering maple"*
*or "Parlor maple"*

**Pentas lanceolata**
*"Egyptian star-cluster"*

**Dimorphotheca ecklonis**
*"Cape marigold"*

**Gerbera jamesonii**
*"African daisy"*
*or "Transvaal daisy"*

**Felicia amelloides**
*"Blue daisy"*

**Ochna serrulata**
*"Mickey-mouse plant"*

**Turnera ulmifolia angustifolia**
*"West Indian holly"*
*or "Sage rose"*

**Feijoa sellowiana**
*"Pineapple guava"*

Medinilla magnifica,
the magnificent "Rose grape"
with showy pink inflorescence

Acalypha hispida (sanderi)
the "Chenille plant" or "Foxtails",
in pendulous cat-tails of bright red flowers

Jacobinia velutina,
the "Brazilian plume", with fountain-like
heads of arched rosy blooms

Strelitzia reginae
*"Bird-of-Paradise"*
*strikingly exotic, from South Africa*

**Cestrum nocturnum**
*"Night jessamine"*

**Gardenia jasminoides 'Fortuniana'**
*"Cape jasmine"*

**Crossandra infundibuliformis**
*"Firecracker flower"*

**Jasminum sambac 'Grand Duke'**
*"Gardenia jasmine"*

**Jasminum sambac**
*"Arabian jasmine"*

**Ervatamia coronaria**
*"Crape jasmine"*

**Lopezia lineata**
*"Mosquito-flower"*

**Beloperone guttata**
*"Shrimp plant"*

**Hedychium gardnerianum**
*"Kahili ginger"*

Hibiscus schizopetalus
*"Japanese lantern"*

Hibiscus rosa-sinensis
'Regius Maximus'
*"Scarlet Chinese hibiscus"*

Hibiscus rosa-sinensis plenus
*"Double rose of China"*

Malvaviscus
penduliflorus (conzatii)
*"Turk's cap"*
*or "Sleepy mallow"*

Datura suaveolens
*"Angel's trumpet"*

Pavonia "intermedia rosea"
*rosy flowers with blue anthers*

Bouvardia ternifolia 'Rosea'
*"Giant pink bouvardia"*

Eranthemum nervosum
*"Blue sage"*

Iochroma tubulosum
*"Violet bush"*

**Raphiolepis indica 'Enchantress'**
*compact "Indian hawthorn"*

**Plumeria rubra acutifolia**
*the "Temple tree" in India*

**Camellia japonica 'Elegans'**
*"Peony camellia"*

**Punica granatum legrellei**
*"Double-flowering pomegranate"*

**Rosa chinensis minima**
*"Pigmy rose" (R. roulettii)*

**Brunfelsia latifolia**
*"Kiss-me-quick"*

**Hebe salicifolia**
*"Evergreen veronica"*

**Carissa acokanthera**
*"Bushman's poison"*

**Viburnum suspensum**
*"Sandankwa viburnum"*

Aphelandra aurantiaca
*"Fiery spike"*

Acacia armata (paradoxa)
*"Kangaroo thorn", for pots*

Aphelandra squarrosa
*"Saffron spike zebra"*

Euphorbia fulgens
*"Scarlet plume"*

Euphorbia pulcherrima
*"Poinsettia"*
*or "Christmas star"*

Adenium obesum
*"Desert rose"*
*or "Impala lily"*

Chorizema cordatum
*"Australian flame pea"*

Callistemon lanceolatus
*"Crimson bottle-brush"*

Erica 'Wilmorei'
*"French heather"*

**Ixora javanica**
*"Jungle geranium"*

**Pachystachys lutea**
*"Gold-hops"*

**Pachystachys coccinea**
*"Cardinal's guard"*

**Cuphea platycentra**
*"Cigar flower"*

**Tibouchina semidecandra**
*"Glory bush"*
or *"Princess flower"*

**Ruellia amoena**
*"Redspray ruellia"*

**Mimulus aurantiacus**
**syn. Diplacus glutinosus**
*"Monkey-flower"*

**Plumbago capensis**
*"Blue Cape plumbago"*

**Clerodendrum x speciosum**
*"Glory-bower"*

# Fruited Holiday Plants

Fruit usually grows on trees or shrubs in orchards or our gardens. But since the time of ancient Egypt in 1530 B.C. and of Babylon in 1137 B.C. man has transplanted fruit trees into containers to bring into gardens or his home. Miniature fruit trees, or plants resembling fruit trees will continue this tradition ideally even in limited space.

Solanum pseudo-capsicum, the "Jerusalem cherry" or "Christmas cherry" loaded in winter with orange-scarlet, cherry-like fruit

Citrus taitensis,
the "Otaheite orange" or "Dwarf orange",
an orange tree in miniature, potgrown for its
fragrant flowers and ornamental golden fruit

Capsicum annuum 'Birdseye',
the "Christmas pepper",
a cheerful Christmas plant covered candle-like
with waxy, berry-like fruits scarlet red.

Citrus mitis, the "Calamondin" orange,
loaded at Christmas time with numerous small
golden-yellow fruits

Pyracantha koidzumii 'Victory',
"Red Fire-thorn", a robust shrub with
long-lasting scarlet berries in winter

Citrus x 'Meyeri', a hybrid of lemon with Sweet orange;
*the "Dwarf Chinese lemon" or "Meyer lemon",*
*with bright yellow lemons for ornament, and delicious for juice*

Fortunella margarita
*"Nagami kumquat"*
*or "Oval kumquat"*

Citrus aurantium
*"Sour Seville orange"*
*bearing freely in containers*

Citrus aurantium myrtifolia
*"Myrtleleaf orange"*
*small leaves and showy fruit*

Citrus limon 'Ponderosa'
*"American wonder-lemon"*
*or "Giant lemon"*

Lycopersicon esculentum 'Tiny Tim'
a miniature "Cherry tomato", with palatable scarlet
fruit; handy in the kitchen window

Citrus paradisi, originally from the West Indies,
"Grapefruit" is now planted in extensive groves for
its juice, but will grow well in large containers also

Musa nana (cavendishii),
the "Chinese dwarf banana" or "Dwarf Jamaica",
of compact habit, and bearing edible deliciously
fragrant, yellow fruit.

Coffea arabica,
the "Arabian coffee tree", in fruit; fragrant white
flowers are followed by crimson berries, each
enclosing two coffee beans.

Passiflora edulis,
the "Purple granadilla", a climber with striking
flowers and edible purple passion fruit.

Ficus carica,
the "Common fig tree" of the Mediterranean region,
much planted for its sweet, pear-shaped "fruit"

**Carissa grandiflora**
*the "Natal plum"*
*fragrant flowers, red fruit*

**Punica granatum nana**
*"Dwarf pomegranate"*
*showy orange-red fruit*

**Olea europaea**
*the "Olive tree"*
*green fruits ripen to black*

**Monstera deliciosa**
*"Mexican breadfruit"*
*fruit with pineapple aroma*

**Ananas comosus (sativus)**
*the cultivated "Pineapple",*
*as a fruited pot plant*

**Cereus peruvianus monstrosus**
*"Peruvian apple cactus"*
*with large, ruby-red fruit*

**Opuntia ficus-indica**
*the "Indian fig"*

**Psidium cattleianum**
*"Strawberry guava"*
*fruit with strawberry flavor*

**Murraya exotica**
*"Orange jessamine"*
*with vivid-red berries*

**Skimmia japonica 'Nana'**
*"Dwarf Japanese skimmia"*
*female plant with red berries*

**Ardisia crispa (crenulata)**
*"Coral berry"*
*scarlet berries long persisting*

**Nertera granadensis (depressa)**
*"Coral-bead plant"*
*or "Hardy baby tears"*

Polyscias fruticosa
the "Ming aralia"
sometimes known as P. filicifolia,
because of its lacy, fern-like foliage.

Fatsia japonica,
the "Japanese aralia"
in horticulture as Aralia sieboldii;
excellent for cooler locations.

Ligustrum lucidum 'Texanum'
*"Wax-leaf privet" in pyramid form*

Brassaia actinophylla, the decorative
"Queensland umbrella tree"
and "Australian schefflera"
of florists, is an effective decorator plant
needing a warm and light location,
and should be kept fairly dry.

**Polyscias filicifolia**
*"Fernleaf aralia"*

**Polyscias guilfoylei victoriae**
*"Lace aralia"*

**Polyscias fruticosa**
*"Ming aralia"*

**Polyscias balfouriana 'Pennockii'**
*"White aralia"*

**Dizygotheca elegantissima**
*"Spider aralia", "Splitleaf maple"*

**Polyscias balfouriana marginata**
*"Variegated Balfour aralia"*

**Pseudopanax lessonii**
*"False panax"*

**Tetrapanax papyriferus**
*"Rice paper plant"*

**Polyscias balfouriana**
*"Dinner plate aralia"*

**Polyscias guilfoylei**
**'Quinquefolia'**
*"Celery-leaved panax"*

**Polyscias fruticasa 'Elegans'**

**Polyscias paniculata 'Variegata'**
*"Variegated rose-leaf panax"*

Ficus benjamina 'Exotica'
*the "Java fig"*
*with gracefully pendant branches*

Ficus stricta
*in Florida as "philippinense";*
*larger foliage than benjamina*

Ficus retusa nitida
*"Indian laurel"*
*in pyramid form*

Ficus retusa, *the "Chinese banyan"*
*as standard trees; very durable*
*as decorators and lending grand decor*

**Ficus religiosa**
*"Sacred Bo-tree" or "Peepul"*

**Ficus krishnae**
*"Sacred fig tree"*

**Ficus sycomorus**
*"Sycamore fig"*

**Ficus rubiginosa variegata**
*"Miniature rubber plant"*

**Ficus elastica 'Doescheri'**
*"Variegated rubber plant"*

**Ficus parcellii**
*"Clown fig"*

**Ficus dryepondtiana**
*"Congo fig"*

**Ficus diversifolia (lutescens)**
*"Mistletoe ficus"*

**Ficus petiolaris**
*"Blue Mexican fig"*

**Ficus lyrata (pandurata)**
*"Fiddleleaf fig"*
*as tubbed combination*

**Ficus benjamina**
*graceful "Weeping fig"*
*in redwood container*

**Pittosporum tobira**
*"Mock-orange" or "Australian laurel"*

**Ficus elastica 'Decora'**
*"Wideleaf rubber plant"*
*combination in tub*

Euonymus japonicus medio-pictus
*"Goldspot euonymus"*

Euonymus jap. aureo-variegatus
*"Yellow Queen"*

Euonymus jap. argenteo-variegatus
*"Silver Queen"*

Euonymus fortunei
radicans gracilis
*"Creeping euonymus"*

Euonymus jap.
microphyllus variegatus
*"Variegated box-leaf"*

Hedera canariensis arb. 'Variegata'
*"Ghost tree ivy"*

Homalocladium platycladum
*"Tapeworm plant"* or *"Ribbon bush"*

Sarcococca ruscifolia
*"Sweet box"*

Myrtus communis microphylla
*"German myrtle"*

Cuphea hyssopifolia
*"False heather"*

Malpighia coccigera
*"Miniature holly"*

Myrsine africana
*"African boxwood"*

x Fatshedera lizei
*"Ivy tree"* or *"Botanical wonder"*

Aucuba japonica variegata
*"Golddust plant"*

Osmanthus heterophyllus
'Variegatus'
*"Variegated false holly"*

Osmanthus fragrans
*"Sweet olive"* or *"Fragrant olive"*

Nerium oleander
'Carneum florepleno'
*"Mrs. Roeding oleander"*
double oleander

Ilex cornuta 'Burfordii'
*"Burford holly"*

Grevillea robusta
*"Silk oak"*

Sparmannia africana
*"Indoor-linden"*
in Oberammergau, Bavaria

Buxus microphylla japonica
*"California boxwood"*

Dracaena deremensis 'Warneckei'
*"Striped dracaena"*

Dracaena fragrans massangeana
*"Cornstalk plant"*

Pleomele reflexa variegata
*"Song of India"*

Dracaena godseffiana
*"Gold-dust dracaena"*

Dracaena sanderiana
*"Ribbon plant"*

Dracaena godseffiana
'Florida Beauty'

Dracaena fragrans 'Victoriae'
*"Painted dragon-lily"*

Dracaena goldieana
*"Queen of dracaenas"*

Dracaena hookeriana
*"Leather dracaena"*

Dracaena marginata
*"Madagascar dragon tree"*
(as floor plant)

Dracaena draco
*"Dragon tree"*

Pleomele thalioides
*"Lance dracaena"*

Dracaena arborea
*"Tree dracaena"*

Cordyline stricta
(Dracaena congesta)

Cordyline terminalis 'Tricolor'
*"Tricolored dracaena"*

Cordyline terminalis var. 'Ti'
*"Good luck plant"* or *"Miracle plant"*

**Pandanus utilis**
*"Screw-pine"*

**Pandanus baptistii**
*"Blue screw-pine"*

**Pandanus veitchii**
*"Variegated screw-pine"*

**Rohdea japonica**
*"Sacred lily of China"*

**Aspidistra elatior (lurida)**
*"Cast-iron plant"*

**Arthropodium cirrhatum**
*"Rock-lily"*

**Chlorophytum comosum
'Variegatum'**
*"Large spider plant" or "Green-lily"*

**Chlorophytum comosum
'Vittatum'**
*"Spider plant"*

**Chlorophytum bichetii**
*"St. Bernard's lily"*

**Clusia rosea**
*"Autograph tree" or "Fat pork tree"*
*with thick-leathery leaves*

**Coccoloba uvifera**
*the "Sea-grape", from tropical shores;*
*red veins in stiff-leathery foliage*

**Bambusa multiplex**
*"Oriental hedge bamboo"*
*a clump-forming type*

**Pseudosasa japonica**
*"Hardy Metake" or "Female arrow bamboo"*
*slowly running and fairly hardy*

Costus malortieanus
'Emerald spiral ginger"

Kaempferia pulchra
"Pretty resurrection lily"

Heliconia illustris
aureo-striata

Heliconia humilis (wagneriana)
"Lobster claw"

Amomum cardamon
"Cardamon ginger"

Alpinia sanderae
"Variegated ginger"

Musa zebrina
"Blood banana"

Musa x paradisiaca
"Common banana"

Musa nana
"Chinese dwarf banana"

**Yucca aloifolia 'Marginata'**
*"Variegated Spanish bayonet"*

**Beaucarnea recurvata**
*"Bottle palm" or "Pony-tail"*

**Yucca elephantipes**
*"Spineless yucca"*

**Dasylirion acrotriche**
*"Bear-grass"*

**Cordyline terminalis 'Negri'**
*"Black dracaena"*

**Hesperaloe parviflora**
*"Western aloe" or "Red yucca"*

**Cordyline australis (juv.)**
*"Cabbage-tree"*

**Phormium tenax 'Variegatum'**
*"Variegated New Zealand flax"*

**Cordyline indivisa 'Rubra'**
*"Red palm-lily"*

Carex foliosissima albo-mediana
*"Miniature variegated sedge"*

Acorus gramineus variegatus
*"Miniature sweet flag"*

Scirpus cernuus (Isolepis)
*"Miniature bulrush"*

Rohdea japonica marginata
*"Sacred Manchu lily"*

Oplismenus hirtellus variegatus
*"Panicum" or "Basket grass"*

Stenotaphrum
secundatum variegatum
*"St. Augustine grass"*

Cyperus alternifolius
*"Umbrella plant"*

Reineckia carnea
*"Fan grass"*

Ophiopogon jaburan 'Variegatus'
*"Variegated Mondo"*

Liriope muscari 'Variegata'
*"Variegated blue lily-turf"*

Ophiopogon jaburan
*"White lily-turf"*

Ophiopogon japonicus
*"Snake's beard"*

Monstera deliciosa, with its picturesque slashed leaves is variously known as "Ceriman", "Mexican Breadfruit", and "Hurricane plant". Where a show plant with exotic accent is required, its giant, dark green foliage, coated with glossy enamel, will always create the most unusual effect.

Monstera obliqua expilata (leichtlinii)
*"Window-leaf"*

**Monstera pertusa**
*formerly known as "Marcgravia paradoxa"*

Known horticulturally and erroneously as "Philodendron pertusum", this is but the juvenile, vining-stage form of Monstera deliciosa. This type is often referred to as "Split-leaf", and "Fruitsalad plant" and its foliage averages smaller than in the mature stage. Cord-like aerial roots either cling to support, or swing free to absorb moisture from the atmosphere.

*Philodendron selloum, a tree philodendron*

*Philodendron bipinnatifidum*

Philodendron eichleri
*"King of Tree-philodendron"*

Philodendron lundii 'Sao Paulo'

Philodendron x barryi

Philodendron sellowianum

Philodendron oxycardium
(cordatum hort.)
*"Heartleaf philodendron"*

Philodendron panduraeforme
*"Fiddle-leaf", "Horsehead",
or "Panda"*

Philodendron squamiferum
*"Red-bristle philodendron"*

Philodendron erubescens
*"Blushing philodendron"*

Philodendron x mandaianum
*"Red-leaf philodendron"*

Philodendron domesticum
(hastatum hort.)
*"Elephant's-ear"*

Philodendron grazielae (fibrillosum)    Philodendron microstictum (pittieri)

Philodendron x 'Florida'

Philodendron lacerum

Philodendron radiatum (dubium)

Philodendron elegans

Philodendron x corsinianum
*"Bronze shield"*

Philodendron melinonii
*"Red birdsnest"*

Philodendron wendlandii
*"Birdsnest philodendron"*

Philodendron cannifolium
*"Flask philodendron"*

Philodendron verrucosum (lindenii)
*"Velvet-leaf"*

Philodendron gloriosum
*"Satin-leaf"*

Philodendron mamei
*"Quilted silver leaf"*

Philodendron x 'Burgundy'

Philodendron sodiroi (juvenile)
*"Silver leaf philodendron"*

Philodendron micans
*"Velvet-leaf vine"*

Philodendron ilsemannii

Philodendron alldreanum
*"Velour philodendron"*

Philodendron melanochrysum
*"Black Gold"*

Anthurium clarinervium
"Hoja de Corazon"

Anthurium veitchii
*"King anthurium"*

Anthurium warocqueanum
*"Queen anthurium"*

Anthurium scandens
*"Pearl anthurium"*

Anthurium crystallinum
*"Crystal anthurium"*

Anthurium hookeri (huegelii)
*"Birdsnest anthurium"*

Spathiphyllum floribundum
(multiflorum)
*"Spathe flower"*

Spathiphyllum 'Clevelandii'
*"White flag"*

Anthurium bakeri

Anthurium **andraeanum** rubrum
*"Wax flower"*

Anthurium x ferrierense
*"Oilcloth-flower"*

Anthurium scherzerianum rothschildianum
*"Variegated Pigtail plant"*

Anthurium scherzerianum
*"Flamingo flower"*, *"Flame plant"*

Aglaonema nitidum 'Curtisii'

Aglaonema crispum
(Schismatoglottis
roebelinii hort.)
*"Painted droptongue"*

Aglaonema commutatum
'White Rajah'
('Pseudo-bracteatum' hort.)
*"Golden evergreen"*

Aglaonema costatum
*"Spotted evergreen"*

Aglaonema pictum

Aglaonema commutatum
'Treubii'
*"Ribbon aglaonema"*

Aglaonema modestum (sinensis)
*"Chinese evergreen"*

Aglaonema 'Silver King'

Aglaonema commutatum
maculatum
*"Silver evergreen"*

Dieffenbachia picta (maculata)
*"Spotted dumbcane"*

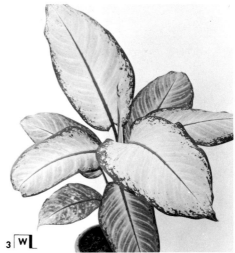

Dieffenbachia picta 'Rud. Roehrs'
*"Gold dieffenbachia"*

Dieffenbachia x bausei

Dieffenbachia leoniae

Dieffenbachia picta 'Superba'
*"Roehrs superba"*

Dieffenbachia amoena
*"Giant dumbcane"*

Scindapsus aureus 'Marble Queen'
*"Taro-vine"*, *"Variegated Philodendron"*

Scindapsus aureus
*"Devil's ivy"*, *"Hunter's robe"*, *"Ivy arum"*,
*commercially known as "Pothos"*

Scindapsus pictus

Scindapsus pictus argyraeus
*"Satin pothos"*

Monstera standleyana
("guttiferyum" hort.)

Homalomena wallisii
*"Silver shield"*

Pothos hermaphroditus
*"True pothos"*

Alocasia cuprea

Alocasia sanderiana
*"Kris plant"*

Colocasia antiquorum illustris
*"Black caladium"*

Rhaphidophora decursiva

Epipremnum pinnatum
("Monstera nechodomii")
*"Taro vine"*

Rhaphidophora celatocaulis
*"Shingle plant"*

Syngonium podophyllum
'Trileaf Wonder'

Syngonium podophyllum
xanthophilum
*"Green Gold"*

Syngonium podophyllum
albolineatum
(Nephthytis triphylla)

Nephthytis gravenreuthii

Xanthosoma lindenii
'Magnificum'

Spathicarpa sagittifolia
*"Fruit-sheath plant"*

Hydrosme rivieri (Amorphophallus)
*"Devil's tongue"*

Caladium 'Ace of Spades'
*"Lance leaf"*

Caladium humboldtii (argyrites)
*"Miniature caladium"*

Caladium 'Lord Derby'
*"Transparent caladium"*

Caladium 'Candidum'
*"White fancy-leaved caladium"*

Caladium 'Frieda Hemple'
*"Red elephant-ear"*

**Ptychosperma elegans**
*the shorter "Solitair" or "Princess palm" (to 20 ft.)*
*Commonly called "Alexander palm"*

**Veitchia merrillii**
*"Christmas palm" or "Manila palm"*

**Caryota mitis**
*suckering "Dwarf fishtail palm"*

**Rhapis excelsa (flabelliformis)**
*the cane-stem "Lady palm" as cluster*

**Chamaedorea erumpens**
*"Bamboo palm"*

**Chamaedorea elegans**
*"Parlor palm"*

**Chamaedorea metallica**
(tenella in hort.)
*"Miniature fishtail"*

**Cycas revoluta**
*"Sago palm", young plant*

**Zamia furfuracea**
*"Jamaica sago-tree"*

**Cycas circinalis**
*"Fern palm"* or *"Crozier cycad"*

**Curculigo capitulata**
*"Palm grass"*
(Amaryllis family)

**Cyclanthus bipartitus**
*"Splitleaf cyclanthus"*
(Cyclanthus family)

**Carludovica palmata**
*"Panama hat plant"*
(Cyclanthus family)

**Chrysalidocarpus lutescens**
*widely known as "Areca palm"*

**Howeia forsteriana**
*popularly known as "Kentia palm"*

**Phoenix canariensis**
*the fresh-green "Canary Islands date palm"*

**Phoenix roebelenii**
*the graceful "Pigmy date" or "Dwarf date palm"*

**Trachycarpus fortunei**
*"Chamaerops excelsa" of horticulture*
*the "Windmill palm"*

**Chamaerops humilis**
*"European fan palm", bushy type*

**Livistona chinensis**
*"Latania borbonica"*
*of horticulture*
*"Chinese fan palm"*

**Syagrus weddelliana**
*in hort. as "Cocos weddelliana"*
*the "Terrarium palm"*

**Sabal palmetto**
*"Cabbage palm", in Florida*

**Coccothrinax argentata**
*"Florida silver palm"*

**Thrinax parviflora**
*"Florida thatch palm"*

**Podocarpus macrophyllus**
*"Buddhist pine"*

**Podocarpus macrophyllus 'Maki'**
*"Southern yew" or "Bamboo-juniper"*

**Podocarpus Nagi**
*"Broadleaf podocarpus"*

**Araucaria bidwillii**
*"Monkey-puzzle" or "Bunya-Bunya"*

**Araucaria heterophylla,**
long known as A. excelsa,
*the "Norfolk Island pine"*

Pinus parviflora (pentaphylla)
*the popular "Japanese white pine".*
*annealed copper wire is used*
*for initial shaping.*

Pinus nigra,
*the "Austrian pine",*
*an early stage bonsai*
*with mat-forming Arenaria verna, the "Irish moss"*

Pinus thunbergii
*the "Japanese black pine"*

Cedrus atlantica glauca
*the "Blue Atlas cedar" 15 yrs. old*

Pinus densiflora
*"Japanese red pine", 100 yrs. old*

Pinus mugo mughus
*"Dwarf Swiss mountain pine"*

**Alsophila cooperi**
*long known in horticulture as "A. australis"*
*"Australian treefern"*

Cibotium schiedei
*"Mexican treefern"*
*in popular 8 inch tub*

Dicksonia squarrosa
*"Rough New Zealand treefern"*

Cibotium chamissoi
**known as "menziesii" in Hawaii,**
*the "Man tree fern", with leathery fronds*

Asplenium nidus
*"Birdsnest fern"*

Polystichum tsus-simense
*"Tsus-sima holly fern"*

Rumohra adiantiformis
(Polystichum coriaceum in hort.)
*"Leather fern"*

Cyrtomium falcatum
*"Fishtail fern"*

Cyrtomium falc. 'Rochfordianum'
*"Holly fern"*

Polystichum aristatum variegatum
*"East Indian holly-fern"*

Pellaea viridis macrophylla
"Pteris adiantoides" in hort.

Pellaea rotundifolia
*"Button fern"*

Pellaea viridis (hastata hort.)
*"Green cliff-brake"*

Nephrolepis biserrata
(ensifolia hort.)
*"Bold sword fern"*

Nephrolepis ex. bostoniensis
compacta
*"Dwarf Boston fern"*

Nephrolepis exaltata 'Whitmanii'
*"Feather fern" or "Lace fern"*

Nephrolepis exaltata
'Fluffy Ruffles'
*"Dwarf feather fern"*

Nephrolepis cordifolia 'Plumosa'
*"Dwarf whitmanii" in hort.*

Nephrolepis exaltata 'Verona'
*"Verona lace fern"*

Nephrolepis exaltata 'Hillii'
*"Crisped featherfern"*

Nephrolepis exaltata
'Rooseveltii plumosa'
*"Tall feather-fern"*

Nephrolepis exaltata
*the ubiquitous "Swordfern"*

**Polypodium vulgare virginianum**
*"Wall fern"*

**Polypodium aureum 'Undulatum'**
*"Blue fern"*

**Asplenium viviparum**
*"Mother fern"*

**Asplenium bulbiferum**
*"Mother spleenwort" or "Hen and chicken fern"*

**Davallia trichomanoides
"canariensis" of horticulture**
*"Carrot fern"*

**Davallia fejeensis plumosa**
*"Dainty rabbit's-foot"*

**Davallia fejeensis**
*"Fiji rabbit's-foot fern"*

**Davallia bullata mariesii**
*"Ball fern"*

**Platycerium bifurcatum**
*"Common staghorn fern"*

**Platycerium willinckii**
*"Silver staghorn fern"*

**Platycerium wilhelminae-reginae**
*"Queen elkhorn"*

**Platycerium coronarium**
*"Crown staghorn"*

Polypodium subauriculatum
*"Jointed pine fern"*

Pòlypodium subauriculatum 'Knightiae'
*"Lacy pine fern"*

Lygodium japonicum
*"Climbing fern"* *(fertile fronds)*

Stenochlaena palustris
*"Liane fern"*

Athyrium filix-foemina
*"Lady fern"*

Aglaomorpha coronans
*"Crowning polypodium"*

Aglaomorpha meyeniana
*"Bear's-paw fern"*

Pteris quadriaurita 'Flabellata'
*"Leather table fern"*

Pteris tremula
*"Trembling brake fern"*

Pteris cretica 'Rivertoniana'
*"Lacy table fern"*

Pteris quadriaurita 'Argyraea'
*"Silver bracken"*

Pteris ensiformis 'Victoriae'
*"Silver table fern"*

Pteris cretica 'Albo-lineata'
*"Variegated table fern"*

Pteris multifida
*"Chinese brake"*

Pteris cretica 'Wilsonii'
*"Fan table fern"*

Pteris cretica 'Wimsettii'
*"Skeleton table fern"*

Pteris dentata
*"Sleepy fern"*

Pteris vittata
in hort. as "longifolia"

Pteris semipinnata
*"Angel-wing fern"*

Adiantum raddianum
'Pacific Maid'

Adiantum tenerum 'Wrightii'
*"Fan maidenhair"*

Adiantum raddianum
"cuneatum" of horticulture
*"Delta maidenhair"*

Polypodium phyllitidis
*"Strap fern"*

Polypodium polycarpon
'Grandiceps'
*"Fishtail"*

Phyllitis scolopendrium
*"Hart's-tongue fern"*

Marsilea drummondii
*"Hairy water clover"*

Azolla caroliniana
*"Mosquito plant" or "Floating moss'*

Ceratopteris thalictroides
*"Water fern"*

Asparagus densiflorus cv. 'Meyers'
*"Plume asparagus"*

Asparagus densiflorus 'Sprengeri'
*"Emerald feather"* or
*"Sprengeri fern"*

Asparagus setaceus
(plumosus in hort.)
*"Asparagus fern"*

Selaginella kraussiana
(denticulata)
*"Club moss"* or
*"Trailing Irish moss"*

Selaginella kraussiana brownii
*"Cushion moss"*

Selaginella emmeliana
*"Sweat plant"*

Selaginella willdenovii
*climbing "Peacock fern"*

Selaginella caulescens
*"Stalked selaginella"*

Selaginella martensii divaricata
*"Zigzag selaginella"*

Sonerila margaritacea
'Mme. Baextele'
*"Frosted sonerila"*

Gynura aurantiaca
*"Velvet plant"*

Stenandrium lindenii

Chamaeranthemum igneum

Crossandra pungens

Ruellia makoyana
*"Monkey plant"*

Pseuderanthemum alatum
*"Chocolate plant"*

Ligularia tussilaginea
aureo-maculata
*"Leopard plant"*

Ligularia tussilaginea argentea
*"Silver farfugium"*

Abutilon striatum
'Aureo-maculatum'
*"Spotted Chinese lantern"*

Abutilon x hybridum
'Souvenir de Bonn'
*"Variegated flowering maple"*

Abutilon striatum thompsonii
*"Spotted flowering maple"*

Hibiscus rosa-sinensis cooperi
*"Checkered hibiscus"*

Acalypha wilkesiana macafeana
*"Copper-leaf"*
*"Match-me-if-you-can"*

Hibiscus rosa-sinensis 'Matensis'
*"Snowflake hibiscus"*

Acalypha wilkesiana obovata
*"Heart copperleaf"*

Abutilon x hybridum 'Savitzii'
*"White parlor-maple"*

Acalypha godseffiana
*"Lance copperleaf"*

Maranta leuconeura kerchoveana
*"Prayer plant"*

Maranta leuconeura massangeana
*"Rabbit's foot"*

Calathea undulata

Maranta leuconeura erythroneura
*"Red-veined prayer plant"*

Calathea argyraea
*"Silver calathea"*

Maranta arundinacea variegata
*"Variegated arrow-root"*

Ctenanthe
lubbersiana

Ctenanthe pilosa (compressa)
*"Giant bamburanta"*

Calathea micans
*"Miniature maranta"*

Calathea roseo-picta

Calathea ornata 'Roseo-lineata'

Calathea insignis
*"Rattlesnake plant"*

Calathea veitchiana

Calathea makoyana
*"Peacock plant"*

Ctenanthe oppenheimiana tricolor
*"Never-never plant"*

Calathea picturata 'Wendlinger'
*also known as 'Argentea'*

Calathea picturata vandenheckei

Calathea louisae

Calathea zebrina
*"Zebra plant"*

Calathea lietzei

Codiaeum 'Mona Lisa'
*"White croton"*

Codiaeum 'L. M. Rutherford'
*"Giant croton"*

Codiaeum 'Elaine'
*"Lance-leaf croton"*

Codiaeum 'Johanna Coppinger'
*"Strap-leaf croton"*

Codiaeum 'Gloriosum superbum'
*"Autumn croton"*

Codiaeum 'Imperialis'
*"Appleleaf croton"*

Codiaeum 'Norwood Beauty'
*"Oakleaf-croton"*

Codiaeum 'Aucubaefolium'
*"Aucuba-leaf"*

Codiaeum 'Punctatum aureum'
*"Miniature croton"*

Peperomia clusiaefolia
*"Red-edged peperomia"*

Peperomia caperata
*"Emerald ripple"*

Peperomia maculosa
*"Radiator plant"*

Peperomia marmorata
*"Silver heart"*

Peperomia sandersii
*"Watermelon peperomia"*

Peperomia verschaffeltii
*"Sweetheart peperomia"*

Peperomia polybotrya
*"Coin leaf peperomia"*

Peperomia griseo-argentea
*"Ivy peperomia"*

Peperomia obtusifolia
*"Baby rubber plant"*

Pilea 'Moon Valley'

**Pilea involucrata**
*"Friendship plant"*

**Breynia nivosa roseo-picta**
*"Leaf flower"*

Pantropic Mimosa pudica, the "Sensitive plant", also known as "Humble plant", "Live and die", "Touch-me-not"; in Vietnam as "Shame plant"; remarkable because its leaflets close and the petioles drop at the slightest touch.

**Dionaea muscipula**
*"Venus fly-trap"*
*jaws snap shut on contact*

Darlingtonia californica, from California and Oregon, the weird "Cobra plant" or "California pitcher plant"; sweet glands in pitchers entice insects to crawl inside

**Sarracenia drummondii**
the showy "Lace trumpets",
apex marbled white

Fittonia verschaffeltii
argyroneura
*"Nerve plant"*

Pilea cadierei
*"Aluminum plant" or*
*"Watermelon pilea"*

Pilea 'Silver Tree' hort.
*"Silver and bronze"*

Peristrophe angustifolia
aureo-variegata
*"Marble-leaf"*

Saxifraga sarmentosa 'Tricolor'
*"Magic carpet"*

Hypoestes sanguinolenta
*"Freckle-face"*

Anoectochilus sikkimensis
*"King of the forest"*
**(Sikkim)**

Bertolonia 'Mosaica'

Hoffmannia roezlii
*"Quilted taffeta plant"*

Graptophyllum pictum
*"Caricature plant"*

Pseuderanthemum reticulatum

Pseuderanthemum atropurpureum
tricolor

Chamaeranthemum venosum

Graptophyllum pictum
albo-marginatum

Chamaeranthemum gaudichaudii

Kaempferia roscoeana
*"Peacock plant"*

Ruellia blumei

Hemigraphis "Exotica" hort.

Scilla violacea
*"Silver squill"*

Justicia extensa

Drimiopsis kirkii

Sanchezia nobilis glaucophylla

Acanthus montanus
*"Mountain thistle"*

Strobilanthes dyerianus
*"Persian shield"*

Manihot esculenta variegata
*"Cassava" or "Tapioca plant"*

Aspidistra elatior 'Variegata'
*"Variegated cast-iron plant"*

x Fatshedera lizei variegata
*"Variegated miracle plant"*

Bougainvillea 'Harrisii'
*"Variegated paper-flower"*

Miconia magnifica
*"Velvet tree"*

Nicodemia diversifolia
*"Indoor oak"*

Trifolium repens minus, in 2 inch pot,
the "Irish shamrock" or "Little white
clover" as sold in America

Oxalis deppei has 4 leaflets; the "Lucky
clover" or "Good luck plant"

Oxalis martiana 'Aureo-reticulata', "Gold-
net sour clover"

Oxalis braziliensis
with rosy flowers

Oxalis bowiei
"Giant pink clover"

Oxalis purpurea (variabilis)
"Grand duchess oxalis"

Oxalis pes-caprae (cernua)
"Bermuda buttercup", with yellow flowers

Oxalis hedysaroides rubra
the "Firefern"

**Hoya carnosa variegata**
*"Variegated wax plant"*

**Hoya carnosa**
*"Wax plant"*

**Hoya bella**
*"Miniature wax plant"*

**Hoya motoskei**
*"Spotted hoya"*

**Hoya australis**
*"Porcelain flower"*

**Hoya purpureo-fusca**
*"Silver-pink vine"*

**Hoya sp. "minima"**
(Dischidia minima hort.)

**Hoya imperialis**
*"Honey plant"*

**Hoya kerrii**
*"Sweetheart hoya"*

Jasminum simplicifolium
*"Little star jasmine"*

Jasminum rex
*"King jasmine"*

Jasminum nitidum
*"Angelwing jasmine"*

Jasminum mesnyi
*"Primrose jasmine"*

Jasminum polyanthum
*"Pink jasmine"*

Jasminum grandiflorum
*"Spanish jasmine"*

Trachelospermum jasminoides
*"Confederate jasmine"*

Stephanotis floribunda
*"Madagascar jasmine"*

Araujia sericofera
*"Bladder flower"*

Passiflora racemosa
*"Red passion flower"*

Passiflora x alato-caerulea
*"Showy passion flower"*

Passiflora caerulea
*"Passion flower"*

**Passiflora coriacea**
*"Bat-leaf"*

Passiflora trifasciata
*"Three-banded passion vine"*

Passiflora maculifolia
*"Blotched-leaf passion vine"*

Passiflora coccinea
*"Scarlet passion flower"*

Passiflora incarnata
*"Wild passion flower"*

Passiflora quadrangularis
*"Granadilla"*

**Cissus rhombifolia**
in hort. as "Vitis" or "Rhoicissus"
*"Grape-ivy"*

**Cissus rhombifolia 'Mandaiana'**
*"Bold grape-ivy"*

**Cissus antarctica**
*"Kangaroo vine"*

**Cissus adenopoda**
*"Pink cissus"*

**Rhoicissus capensis**
*"Evergreen grape"*

**Cissus rotundifolia**
*"Arabian wax cissus"*

**Piper nigrum**
*"Black pepper"*

**Cissus discolor**
*"Rex begonia vine"*

**Piper ornatum**
*"Celebes pepper"*

Plectranthus purpuratus
*"Moth king"*

Plectranthus oertendahlii
*"Prostrate coleus"*

Plectranthus australis
*"Swedish ivy"*

Pellionia daveauana
*"Trailing watermelon begonia"*

Plectranthus coleoides
'Marginatus'
*"Candle plant"*

Pellionia pulchra
*"Satin pellionia"*

Senecio mikanioides
*"German ivy"*

Thunbergia alata
*"Black-eyed Susan"*

Manettia inflata (bicolor)
*"Firecracker plant"*

Pothos jambea

Hemigraphis colorata
*"Red ivy"*

Saxifraga sarmentosa
*"Strawberry geranium"*

Zebrina pendula
*"Silvery wandering Jew"*

Tradescantia sillamontana
*"White velvet"*
*"White gossamer"*

Tradescantia fluminensis
'Variegata'
*"Variegated wandering Jew"*

Zebrina purpusii
*"Bronze wandering Jew"*

Zebrina pendula 'Discolor'
*"Tricolor wandering Jew"*

Setcreasea purpurea
*"Purple heart"*

Callisia elegans
*"Striped inch plant"*

Cyanotis somaliensis
*"Pussy-ears"*

Cyanotis kewensis
*"Teddy-bear vine"*

Dichorisandra thyrsiflora
*"Blue ginger"*

Callisia fragrans 'Melnikoff'
(Spironema in hort.)

Gibasis geniculata
(Tradescantia multiflora in hort.)
*"Tahitian bridal veil"*

**Siderasis fuscata**
*"Brown spiderwort"*

**Callisia fragrans**
(Tradescantia dracaenoides)

**Hadrodemas warszewicziana**
(Tripogandra or Spironema)

**Dichorisandra thyrsiflora
variegata**

**Campelia zanonia 'Mexican Flag'**
(Dichorisandra albo-lineata)

**Dichorisandra reginae**
*"Queen's spiderwort"*

**Ipomoea batatas 'Blackie'**
*"Black-leaf sweet-potato"*

**Geogenanthus undatus**
*"Seersucker plant"*

**Palisota elizabethae**

**Rhoeo spathacea (discolor)**
*"Moses-in-the-cradle"*

**Gynura bicolor**
*"Oakleaved velvet plant"*

**Gynura 'Sarmentosa' hort.**
*"Purple passion vine"*

**Lamium galeobdolon variegatum**
*"Silver nettle vine" or "Archangel"*

**Coleus rehneltianus
'Trailing Queen'**
*"Trailing coleus"*

**Vinca major variegata**
*"Band plant"*

**Helxine soleirolii**
*"Baby's tears"*

**Pilea microphylla (muscosa)**
*"Artillery plant"*

**Mentha requienii**
*"Corsican mint"*

**Ficus radicans 'Variegata'**
*"Variegated rooting fig"*

**Ficus pumila**
*"Creeping fig"*

**Ficus tikoua**
*"Waupahu fig"*

**Pilea nummulariifolia**
*"Creeping Charlie"*

**Glecoma hederacea variegata**
*"Variegated ground-ivy"*

**Cymbalaria muralis**
*"Kenilworth ivy"*

Gloriosa rothschildiana
*"Glory-lily"*

Gloriosa carsonii

Ceropegia woodii
*"String of hearts"*

Wedelia trilobata

Mikania ternata
*"Plush vine"*

Browallia speciosa alba
*"White bush-violet"*

Campanula isophylla mayii
*"Italian bellflower"*

Schizocentron elegans
*"Spanish shawl"*

Peperomia scandens 'Variegata'
*"Variegated philodendron leaf"*

**Dioscorea bulbifera**
*"Air-potato" or "True yam"*

**Streptosolen jamesonii**
*"Marmalade bush" or "Firebush"*

**Tolmiea menziesii**
*"Piggy-back plant"*

**Bowiea volubilis**
*"Climbing onion"*

**Bougainvillea glabra**
*"Paper flower"*

**Clerodendrum thomsonae**
*"Bleeding-heart vine"*

**Dipladenia sanderi**
*"Rose dipladenia"*

**Allamanda cathartica hendersonii**
*"Golden trumpet"*

**Hedera helix**
*"English ivy"*

**Hedera helix 'Albany'**
*"Albany ivy"*

**Hedera helix 'Pittsburgh'**
*"Pittsburgh ivy"*

**Hedera helix 'Patricia'**
*a dense, selfbranching ivy*

**Hedera canariensis 'Variegata'**
*"Variegated Algerian ivy"*

**Hedera helix 'Harald'**
*"White and green ivy"*
*"Improved Chicago variegata"*

**Hedera colchica**
**'Dentato-variegata'**
*"Variegated Persian ivy"*

**Hedera can. 'Gloire de Marengo'**
*in Boskoop, Holland*

**Espostoa lanata**
*"Peruvian old man"*

**Cephalocereus senilis**
*"Old man cactus"*

**Oreocereus celsianus**
*"Old man of the Andes"*

**Cleistocactus straussii**
*"Silver torch"*

**Lobivia aurea (Pseudolobivia)**
*"Golden lily-cactus"*

**Lemaireocereus beneckei**
*"Silver tip", "Chalk candle"*

**Echinopsis multiplex**
*"Easter-lily cactus"*

**Rebutia kupperiana**
*"Red crown"*

**Echinocereus purpureus**
*"Purple hedgehog"*

Cereus "peruvianus" hort.
popular "Column-cactus"

Myrtillocactus geometrizans
*"Blue myrtle" tree cactus*

Trichocereus pachanoi
*"Night-blooming San Pedro"*

Cereus hexagonus
*"South American blue column"*

Mammillaria magnimamma
*"Mexican pincushion"*

Mammillaria geminispina (bicolor)
*"Whitey"*

Mammillaria bocasana
*"Powder puff"*

Mammillaria compressa
*"Mother of hundreds"*

Mammillaria elongata
*"Golden stars"*

Mammillaria fragilis
*"Thimble-cactus"*

Opuntia rufida
*"Cinnamon-cactus"*

Opuntia microdasys
*"Bunny ears"*

Opuntia microdasys
albispina
*"Polka-dots"*

Opuntia basilaris
*"Beaver tail"*

Opuntia subulata
*"Eve's-pin cactus"*

Opuntia vilis
*"Little tree-cactus"*

Opuntia cylindrica
*"Emerald idol"*

Opuntia leucotricha
*"White-hair tree-cactus"*

Parodia sanguiniflora violacea
*"Crimson Tom thumb"*

G. mihan. friedrichii 'Rubra' (grafted)
*"Oriental Moon" cactus*

Gymnocalycium mihanovichii
*"Plain chin-cactus"*

Astrophytum capricorne
*"Goat's-horn"*

Astrophytum asterias
*"Sand dollar"*

Astrophytum myriostigma
*"Bishop's cap"*

Leuchtenbergia principis
*"Prism-cactus", "Agave cactus"*

Echinocactus grusonii
*"Golden barrel"*

Notocactus haselbergii
*"White-web ball"*

Hamatocactus setispinus
*"Strawberry-cactus"*

Ferocactus latispinus
*"Fish-hook barrel"*

Notocactus rutilans
*"Pink ball"*

**Opuntia tomentosa (velutina)**
*"Velvet opuntia"*

**Opuntia vulgaris variegata**
*"Joseph's coat"*

**Opuntia ficus-indica 'Burbank'**
*"Spineless Indian fig"*

**Opuntia schickendantzii**
*"Lion's tongue"*

**Opuntia vulgaris (monacantha)**
*"Irish mittens"*

**Opuntia brasiliensis**
*"Tropical tree-opuntia"*

**Opuntia linguiformis 'Maverick'**
*"Maverick cactus"*

**Opuntia erinacea ursina**
*"Grizzly bear"*

**Opuntia fulgida
mamillata monstrosa**
*"Boxing-glove"*

Epiphyllum hybrid 'Elegantissimum'
*"Dwarf orchid cactus"*

Epiphyllum x hybridus
*"Orchid cactus"*

Nopalxochia ackermannii
x 'Fire Glory'

Epiphyllum oxypetalum
*"Queen of the night"*

Nopalxochia phyllanthoides
*"German Empress"*

Rhipsalis cassutha
*"Mistletoe-cactus"*

Selenicereus grandiflorus
*"Queen of the Night"*

Hylocereus undatus
*"Honolulu queen"*

Harrisia tortuosa
*"Red-tipped
dog-tail"*

Cleistocactus smaragdiflorus
*"Firecracker-cactus"*

Nyctocereus serpentinus
*"Snake-cactus"*

Acanthocereus
pentagonus
*"Big-needle vine"*

Lophophora williamsii, the "Sacred
mushroom" or "Peyote", having
narcotic properties, and revered
by Indians

Pereskia grandifolia, a "Rose cactus", with true leaves, a living
image of the ancestors of the
cactus family that lived millions
of years ago

Chamaecereus silvestri
*"Peanut-cactus"*

Rhipsalidopsis rosea
*"Dwarf Easter-cactus"*

Schlumbergera bridgesii
*"Christmas cactus"*

Rhipsalidopsis x graeseri 'Rosea'
(Epiphyllopsis)

Rhipsalidopsis gaertneri
*"Easter cactus"*

Rhipsalidopsis x graeseri
(Epiphyllopsis)

Zygocactus truncatus delicatus
*"White crab-cactus"*

Zygocactus truncatus
*"Thanksgiving cactus", "Crab-cactus"*

Schlumbergera russelliana
*"Shrimp cactus"*

**Agave ferdinandi-regis**
*the shapely, very beautiful "King agave"*

**Agave victoriae-reginae**
*"Queen Victoria agave",*
*a very formal, small rosette*

**Agave potatorum**
*"Drunkard agave"*

**Agave angustifolia marginata**
*"Variegated Caribbean agave"*

**Agave filifera**
*"Thread agave"*

**Aloe brevifolia**
A. "humilis" of the trade

**Aloe brevifolia depressa**
*"Crocodile jaws"*

**Aloe striata**
*"Coral aloe"*

**Aloe saponaria**
*"Soap aloe"*

**Aloe vera chinensis**
*"Indian medicine aloe"*

**Aloe x humvir**
*"Needle-aloe"*

**Crassula rupestris**
*"Rosary vine"*

**Crassula periorata 'Pagoda'**
*"Pagoda plant"*

**Crassula perfossa**
*"String o' buttons"*

**Crassula lactea**
*"Tailor's patch"*

**Crassula cultrata**
*"Propeller plant"*

**Crassula pseudolycopodioides**
*"Princess pine"*

**Aeonium haworthii**
*"Pin-wheel"*

**Aeonium 'Pseudo-tabulaeforme'**
*"Green platters"*

**Aeonium arboreum
atropurpureum**
*"Black tree aeonium"*

**Adromischus festivus**
*"Plover eggs"*

**Kalanchoe tomentosa**
*"Panda plant"*

**Adromischus maculatus**
*"Calico hearts"*

Aloe variegata, "Tiger aloe"
Stapelia hirsuta, "Hairy toad plant"
Gasteria verrucosa, "Wart gasteria"

Agave decipiens, "False sisal"
Agave striata 'Nana', "Lilliput agave"
Aloe arborescens, "Octopus plant"

Kalanchoe marmorata, "Pen wiper"
Senecio serpens, "Blue chalk sticks"
Kalanchoe 'Roseleaf', (beharensis x tomentosa)

Euphorbia lactea, "Candelabra plant"
Sansevieria 'Hahnii', "Birdsnest"
Euphorbia splendens, "Crown of thorns"

Aeonium decorum, "Copper pinwheel"
Kalanchoe tomentosa, "Panda plant"
Echeveria multicaulis, "Copper roses"

Kalanchoe fedtschenkoi, "Purple scallops"
Cotyledon barbeyi, "Hoary navelwort"
Crassula tetragona, "Miniature pine tree"

Gibbaeum petrense, "Flowering quartz"
Lithops marmorata, "Living stone"
Dinteranthus wilmotianus, "Split rock"

Pleiospilos nelii, "Cleft stone"
Titanopsis calcarea, "Limestone mimicry"
Pleiospilos bolusii, "Living rock cactus"

Crassula argentea, "Jade plant"
Crassula arborescens, "Silver dollar"
Crassula rupestris, "Rosary vine"

Crassula 'Tricolor Jade', "Tricolored jade plant"
Portulacaria afra variegata, "Rainbow bush"
Crassula dubia; "obvallata" hort.

Pachyphytum 'Cornelius', "Moonstones"
Sedum adolphii, "Golden sedum"
Pachyphytum compactum, "Thick plant"

Kalanchoe fedtschenkoi 'Marginata', "Aurora Borealis"
Sedum rubrotinctum, "Christmas cheers"
Graptopetalum paraguayense, "Ghost plant"

Sempervivum tectorum calcareum, "Houseleek"
Euphorbia mammillaris, "Corncob cactus"
Faucaria tigrina, "Tiger jaws"

Echeveria elegans, "Mexican snowball"
Echeveria derenbergii, "Painted lady"
Echeveria 'Pulv-oliver', "Plush plant"

Aloe nobilis, "Gold-tooth-aloe"
Aloe humilis 'Globosa', "Spider aloe"
Aloe brevifolia depressa, "Crocodile jaws"

x Gasterhaworthia 'Royal Highness'
Haworthia subfasciata, "Little zebra plant"
x Gastrolea 'Spotted Beauty', "Gasteria-aloe hybrid"

Echeveria peacockii var. subsessilis
*desmetiana    hort.*

Echeveria elegans
*"Mexican snowball" or "Mexican gem"*

Echeveria gilva
*"Wax rosette"*

Echeveria glauca
*"Blue echeveria"*

x Sedeveria derenbergii
*"Baby echeveria"*

x Pachyveria 'Curtis'
*"White cloud"*

Haworthia margaritifera
*"Pearl plant"*

Haworthia fasciata
*"Zebra haworthia"*

Haworthia cuspidata
*"Star window plant"*

x Gastrolea beguinii
*"Pearl aloe" or "Lizard-tail"*

Haworthia papillosa
*"Pearly dots"*

Gasteria x'Hybrida'
*"Oxtongue" or "Bowtie-plant"*

Euphorbia ingens
*"Candelabra tree"*

Euphorbia lactea
*"Candelabra cactus"*

Euphorbia trigona
in hort. as "hermentiana"
*"African milk tree"*

Euphorbia polyacantha
*"Fish bone cactus"*

Euphorbia mammillaris
*"Corncob cactus"*

Euphorbia mammillaris 'Variegata'
*"Indian corn cob"*

Euphorbia lactea cristata
*'Elkhorn" or "Frilled fan"*

Euphorbia tirucalli
*"Milk bush" or "Pencil cactus"*

Euphorbia splendens bojeri
*"Dwarf crown-of-thorns"*

Kalanchoe pinnata (Bryophyllum)
*"Airplant" or "Miracle leaf"*
sprouting plantlets on leaves

Kalanchoe gastonis-bonnieri
*"Life plant" with young plants at leaf tips*

Sedum morganianum
*"Burro tail" in basket*

Senecio macroglossus variegatus
*"Variegated wax-ivy"*

Senecio jacobsenii (petraeus)
*"Weeping notonia"*

Pleiospilos simulans
*"African living rock"*

Faucaria tuberculosa
*"Pebbled tiger jaws"*

Fenestraria rhopalophylla
*"Baby toes"*

**Stapelia variegata**
*"Carrion flower" or "Spotted toad cactus"*

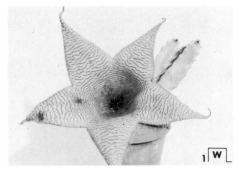

**Stapelia gigantea**
*"Giant toad plant" or "Zulu giants"*

**Caralluma nebrownii**
*"Spiked clubs"*

**Tavaresia grandiflora**
*"Thimble flower"*

**Huernia zebrina**
*"Owl eyes"*

**Lithops pseudotruncatella**
*a "Living stone"*

**Lithops karasmontana**
*"Mountain pebble"*

**Lithops bella**
*"Pretty stone face"*

**Rhombophyllum dolabriforme**
*"Hatchet plant" (Collection Marnier-Lapostolle)*

**Rhombophyllum nelii (Hereroa hort.)**
*"Elkhorns", (Marnier-Lapostolle, France)*

**Sansevieria trifasciata 'Hahnii'**
*"Birdsnest sansevieria"*

**Sans. trifasciata 'Golden hahnii'**
*"Golden birdsnest"*

**Sansevieria trifasciata laurentii**
*"Variegated snake plant"*

**Sansevieria intermedia**
*"Pygmy bowstring"*

**Sansevieria guineensis**
*"Bowstring hemp"*

**Sansevieria cylindrica**
*"Spear sansevieria"*

**Sansevieria ehrenbergii**
*"Blue sansevieria" or "Seleb"*

**Sansevieria senegambica**
**"cornui" in hort.**

**Sansevieria grandis**
*"Grand Somali hemp"*

**Sansevieria trifasc.**
**'Bantel's Sensation'**
*"White sansevieria"*

**Sansevieria "Kirkii" hort.**
*"Star sansevieria"*

**Sansevieria zeylanica**
*"Devil's tongue"*
*true species from Ceylon*

**Combination Text-Index:** Numerals at end of each listing indicate page numbers to plant illustrations, a short-cut to easier finding of photographs (* denotes in color).

**Plant Names** other than species, in conformance with the International Code of Nomenclature, are generally distinguished as follows:

**Names of Hybrids:** Generic names of bigeneric hybrids, and Latinized specific names of hybrids derived from two species, are as a rule preceded by the x mark;

**Cultivar names** (horticultural sports or varieties, hybrids with fancy names and clonal selections) start with a capital initial letter, and are enclosed within single quotation marks (');

**Names of uncertain standing,** or where incorrectly used in horticulture, are shown in double quotes (''), and/or are followed by the abbreviation "hort".

**Guide to Plant requirements and care** for each plant will be found with individual plant photos in form of pictograph symbols, explained in detail on pages 10 and 11. Quick reference Key to Care can be found at end of book.

**Terms of measurement** are generally given according to the International Metric System. Conversions to the Old English terms are:

1 centimeter (cm) = 0.4 inch;   $2\frac{1}{2}$ cm = 1 inch;   10 cm = 4 inches
1 meter (m) = 40 inches (or 3.28 feet). (1 cm = 10 mm; 1 m = 100 cm; 1 foot = 30 cm)
1 gram (g) = 0.035 oz; 1 kilogram (kg) = 2.2 lbs; 1 liter (1) = 1.06 quarts; 4 liters = 1.06 gal.

**Temperature Conversion:** Degrees Fahrenheit vs. Centigrade.
Freezing point zero deg. Centigrade = 32 deg. Fahrenheit (F.).
Boiling point 100 deg. Celsius (C) = 212 deg. Fahrenheit (F.).

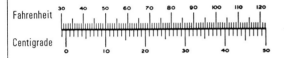

Fahrenheit

Centigrade

Inches

Millimeters

Centimeters

---

**ABUTILON** (*Malvaceae*)

**x hybridum,** (American tropics). "Flowering maple'; pubescent foliage; yellow to red bell-like flowers all year 5 cm long; white, yellow, salmon or red. p. 62

**x hybridum 'Savitzii',** "White parlor-maple"; Colorful foliage grayish-green variegated white. p. 115

**x hybridum 'Souvenir de Bonn',** "Variegated flowering maple"; grayish leaves bordered white; flowers salmon, veined with crimson. p. 115

**megapotamicum variegatum,** "Weeping Chinese lantern"; drooping branches; leaves variegated yellow; yellow 5 cm flowers, lantern-like red calyx. p. 62

**striatum 'Aureo-maculatum',** "Spotted Chinese lantern"; fol. blotched yellow; orange bell-flowers. p. 115

**striatum thompsonii** (Guatemala), "Spotted flowering maple"; mottled chartreuse-yellow leaves not hairy; bell-like orange-salmon flowers; good houseplant. p. 115

**ACACIA** (*Leguminosae*)

**armata** (paradoxa) (Australia), "Kangaroo thorn"; dark green, spiny; 1 cm yellow flowers in spring. p. 67

**ACALYPHA** (*Euphorbiaceae*)

**godseffiana** (New Guinea), "Lance copperleaf"; green leaves with serrate cream margins. p. 115

**hispida** (Sanderi) (India), "Chenille plant" or "Foxtails"; bright crimson flowers in pendant spikes resembling tassels; bright green, hairy leaves. p. 5, 63

**wilkesiana macafeana** .(New Hebrides), "Copperleaf"; large red leaves marbled crimson and bronze, 12–20 cm long; very colorful shrub, needs sun. p. 115

**wilkesiana obovata** (Polynesia), "Heart copperleaf"; leaves green edged cream, changing to copper. p. 115

**ACANTHOCEREUS** (*Cactaceae*)

**pentagonus** (Caribbean), "Big-needle vine"; night-blooming with large white flowers. p. 142

**ACANTHUS** (*Acanthaceae*)

**montanus** (West Africa), "Mountain thistle"; lobed, black-green, spiny 30 cm leaves; flowers white. p. 123

**ACHIMENES** (*Gesneriaceae*)

**ehrenbergii** (Mexico); white woolly plant; 4 cm slipper flowers orchid, with white throat marked purple. p. 49

**erecta** (coccinea) (Jamaica), "Cupid's bower"; trailing stems with hairy leaves, 3 cm intense scarlet flowers in profusion. A pretty miniature. p. 49

**longiflora 'Andersonii',** "Trumpet achimenes"; stiff-hairy foliage; 6 cm purple flowers; forms rhizomes. p. 49

**ACORUS** (*Araceae*)

**gramineus variegatus** (Japan), "Miniature sweet flag"; 10 to 30 cm fan of leathery leaves, light green and variegated white; terrarium plant. p. 86

**ADENIUM** (*Apocynaceae*)

**obesum** (East Africa), "Desert rose" or "Impala lily"; succulent bush; showy 5 cm flowers pinkish, edged carmine, fleshy leaves glossy green. p. 67

**ADIANTUM** (*Filices*)

**raddianum;** "cuneatum" of horticulture (Brazil), "Delta maidenhair"; sturdy fronds with small green leaflets, 20–40 cm long; fairly tolerant as houseplant. p. 112

**raddianum 'Pacific Maid'** (Peru); of compact habit with stiffish fronds of large green leaflets. p. 112

**tenerum 'Wrightii'** (West Indies), "Fan maidenhair"; firm fronds pink when young. p. 112

**ADROMISCHUS** (*Crassulaceae*)

**festivus** (So. Africa), "Plover eggs"; succulent silvery leaves marbled maroon. p. 145

**maculatus** (So. Africa), "Calico hearts"; succulent gray-green leaves flecked red-brown. p. 145

**AECHMEA** (*Bromeliaceae*)

**x 'Bert';** green leaf rosette with purplish crossbands; dense head of red bracts and pale flowers. p. 42

**caudata variegata** (Brazil), "Billbergia forgetii" in hort.; stiff green leaves banded cream; bracts lemon, sheathing golden flowers in bold cluster. cover, p. 41

**chantinii** (Amazonas), "Amazonian zebra plant"; striking olive-green rosette with gray crossbands; inflorescence with red bracts and yellow flowers. p. 41

**fasciata** (Brazil), "Silver vase"; tigered silver-white; durable inflorescence of rosy bracts. cover, p. 9, 42

**x 'Fosters Favorite',** "Lacquered wine-cup"; wine-red rosette; pendulous spike with red berries. p. 42

**fulgens** (Brazil), "Coral berry"; leaves dusted gray; showy cluster with red berries; flower purple. p. 42

**fulgens discolor** (Brazil); olive-green rosette with purple underside; showy cluster of oval red berries tipped by violet flowers. (cover)

**mariae-reginae** (Costa Rica), "Queen aechmea"; gray leaves; spike with pink bracts and red-tipped berries. p. 42

**153**

**squarrosa** (Brazil), "Saffron spike zebra"; glossy leaves veined white; waxy golden yellow bracts. p. 67
**squarrosa 'Louisae'** (Brazil); compact "Zebra plant"; dark leaves with white veins; golden bracts. p. 9

**ARAUCARIA** (*Araucariaceae*)
**bidwillii** (Queensland), "Monkey-puzzle" or "Bunya-Bunya"; vicious-looking with broad, glossy, sharp-pointed needles. p. 103
**heterophylla** (South Pacific), long known in horticulture as A. excelsa, the "Norfolk Island pine"; soft, awl-shaped needles. Handsome, formal shape; good houseplant. p. 103

**ARAUJIA** (*Asclepiadaceae*)
**sericofera** (So. Brazil), "Bladder flower"; fragrant flowers 2½ cm dia., white or pinkish. p. 126

**ARDISIA** (*Myrsinaceae*)
**crispa** (crenulata) (Japan to Malaya), "Coral berry"; shining leathery leaves; fragrant flowers followed by scarlet berries. p. 72

**ARTHROPODIUM** (*Liliaceae*)
**cirrhatum** (New Zealand), "Rock-lily"; flexible light green leaves; white flowers. p. 82

**ASPARAGUS** (*Liliaceae*)
**densiflorus cv. 'Meyers'** (So. Africa), "Plume asparagus"; charming green spindles. p. 113
**densiflorus 'Sprengeri'** (Natal), "Emerald feather" or "Sprengeri fern"; fluffy with soft green needles. p. 113
**setaceus** (plumosus in hort.) (So. Africa), "Asparagus fern"; lacy fronds in horizontal plane. p. 113

**ASPIDISTRA** (*Liliaceae*)
**elatior** (lurida) (China), "Cast-iron plant"; tough-leathery foliage shining deep green. p. 82
**elatior 'Variegata'**, "Variegated cast-iron plant"; attractive with leaves striped green and white. p. 123

**ASPLENIUM** (*Filices*)
**bulbiferum** (New Zealand to Malaya), "Mother spleenwort"; arching fronds bearing bulbils or plantlets. p. 108
**nidus** (India to Queensland), "Birdsnest fern"; epiphytic rosette of shining, friendly green fronds. p. 106
**viviparum** (Mauritius), "Mother fern"; lacy fronds giving rise to tiny bulblets. p. 108

**ASTILBE** (*Saxifragaceae*)
**japonica 'Gladstone'**, the florists "Spiraea"; perennial with plumes of white flowers. p. 25

**ASTROPHYTUM** (*Cactaceae*)
**asterias** (No. Mexico), "Sand dollar"; coppery with white scales; flowers yellow w. red throat. p. 139
**myriostigma** (C. Mexico), "Bishop's cap"; small globe to 20 cm dia., covered with white spots. p. 139

**ATHYRIUM** (*Filices*)
**filix-foemina** (Arctic and Temp. zones), "Lady fern"; graceful feathery, herbaceous fronds. p. 110

**AUCUBA** (*Cornaceae*)
**japonica variegata** (Himalayas to Japan), "Golddust plant"; leathery leaves dark green, blotched yellow. p. 79

**AZALEA** (*Ericaceae*)
**'Coral Bells'** (Japanese Kurume hybrid); small hose-in-hose flowers dainty silver pink. p. 14
**'Hoxo'** (simsii hyb.), "Dwarf Azalea indica"; free-blooming with flowers glowing crimson. p. 14, 15

**AZOLLA** (*Filices*)
**caroliniana** (U.S. to Argentina), "Mosquito plant" or "Floating moss"; aquatic bodies 2 cm long pale green to reddish. p. 112

**BAMBUSA** (*Gramineae*)
**multiplex** (Vietnam), "Oriental hedge bamboo"; reed-like hollow stems with fern-like leaves. p. 83

**BEAUCARNEA** (*Liliaceae*)
**recurvata** (Mexico), "Bottle palm" or "Pony-tail"; crown of leaves on trunk with swollen base. p. 85

**BEGONIA** (*Begoniaceae*)
**x 'Alto-Scharff'**; white-hairy leaves red beneath. p. 36
**x argenteo-guttata**, "Trout-begonia"; angelwings olive green spotted silver; red beneath. p. 33
**bartonea** (Puerto Rico), "Winter jewel"; green leaves overcast with gem-like sheen; pink blossoms. p. 37
**boweri** (So. Mexico), "Miniature eyelash begonia"; vivid green with blackish patches. p. 5, 35
**bradei** (Brazil); soft-hairy, velvety olive green w. red margins; flowers white with crimson hairs. p. 36
**x 'Braemar'**; white-hairy stems with lustrous green leaves, glossy red beneath; bearded flowers white. p. 36
**x cheimantha 'Lady Mac'**, "Christmas begonia"; covered in winter with masses of long-lasting pink fl. p. 24
**x 'Cleopatra'**, "Mapleleaf begonia"; foliage nile-green with chocolate areas toward margin; pink flowers. p. 39

**coccinea** (Brazil), an "Angelwing begonia"; tall to 5 m; leaves glossy green spotted silver; fl. coral-red. p. 33
**x 'Corallina de Lucerna'**; olive green angelwing fol. spotted silver; wine-red beneath. p. 33
**x credneri**; white-hairy leaves olive green, red beneath; bearded flowers pink. p. 37
**egregia** (Brazil); light green, puckered leaves somewhat cupped; flowers white. p. 35
**x 'Elsie M. Frey'**; a basket plant; metallic green, red-lined leaves; fragrant pink flowers. p. 40
**eminii** (mannii) (W. Africa), "Roseleaf begonia"; glossy green leaves pale beneath; fl. white streaked red. p. 35
**epipsila** (Brazil); fleshy, roundish, enamel-green foliage, red-felted beneath; white flowers. p. 37
**x erythrophylla 'Bunchii'**, "Curly kidney begonia"; curious mutant w. fleshy leaves red-tinged and crested. p. 38
**x erythrophylla helix**, "Whirlpool begonia"; fleshy leaves spiralled like corkscrew in center. p. 38
**fernandoi-costa** (Brazil); soft-hairy bright green fol., rosy beneath; flowers white. p. 34
**x fuscomaculata**; hairy plant with smooth, bronzy leaves spotted chocolate, flowers pink. p. 38
**goegoensis** (Sumatra), "Fire king begonia"; exquisite with silky leaves dark bronze with lighter veins; fl. pink. p. 39
**heracleifolia** (Mexico), "Star begonia"; bristly, palmate leaves bronzy with green patches; fl. pink. p. 38
**heracleifolia nigricans** (Mexico); leaves blackish-green with contrasting pale green areas. p. 38
**x hiemalis 'Apricot Beauty'**, "Apricot winter begonia"; semi-tuberous, with salmon-pink flowers which will drop if kept too warm and dry. p. 24
**x hiemalis 'Rieger's Schwabenland'**; robust, with glowing scarlet fl. to 5 cm dia., superior keep. quality. p. 23
**hispida cucullifera** (Sao Paulo), "Piggyback begonia"; velvety fol. producing adventitious leaflets on surface p. 34
**hydrocotylifolia** (Mexico), "Miniature pond-lily"; thick, waxy 5 cm leaves light olive; rosy fl. p. 34
**'Immense'** (ricinifolia seedling); light green, waxy leaves edged red; fl. pink. p. 38
**imperialis** (Mexico), "Carpet begonia"; dwarf, hairy pl. with pebbly leaves bronzy with lighter areas. p. 39
**incana** (Mexico); woolly-white plant with fleshy leaves; pendant white flowers. p. 36
**involucrata** (Costa Rica); velvety green leaves lightly white-hairy; fl. white and fragrant. p. 37
**kellermannii** (Guatemala); cupped leaves yellow-green to rose; white-felted beneath; flowers pink. p. 36
**leptotricha** (Paraguay), "Woolly bear"; dark green thickish leaves, brown felted beneath; fl. ivory. p. 36
**limmingheiana** (glaucophylla) (Brazil), "Shrimp begonia"; trailer with glossy leaves; coral-red flowers. p. 40
**manicata 'Aureo-maculata crispa'**, "Crisped leopard begonia"; waxy leaves blotched yellow. p. 38
**x margaritacea**; distinctive hybrid with metallic, purplish leaves overlaid with silver; fl. pink. p. 35
**x margaritae**; bushy with soft white-hairy, bronze leaves; fl. pink w. red whiskers. p. 37
**masoniana** (S.E. Asia), "Iron cross begonia"; beautiful with large leaves nile green marked boldly with brown, waxy flowers greenish with maroon bristles. p. 5, 9, 39
**metallica** (Brazil), "Metallic-leaf begonia"; bushy silver-hairy pl. with olive green leaves; bristly pink fl. p. 37
**'Nelly Bly'**; hairy plant with quilted, dark green leaves, red beneath; bearded flowers pink. p. 37
**'Pink Parade'**; angelwings waxy bronze thickly silver-spotted; flowers shrimp-pink. p. 33
**pustulata** (Mexico), "Blister begonia"; beautiful pebbly leaves off-emerald green with silver veins. p. 39
**rex 'Comtesse Louise Erdoedy'**, "Corkscrew begonia"; red-hairy spiralled foliage lt. olive, zoned with silver. p. 40
**rex 'Helen Teupel'**, "Diadema hybrid"; deeply laced leaves patterned fuchsia-red, metallic green, sil.-pink. p. 40
**rex 'Merry Christmas'**; gaily zoned leaf blackish-red, shimmering ruby, silver and pink, green and red. p. 5, 40
**rex 'Peace'**; robust cultivar; center metallic red, bal. silvery with pink sheen. p. 9
**rex 'President'** ('Pres. Carnot'); sturdy old hyb.; quilted leaf moss-green, raised areas silver. p. 40
**x ricinifolia**, "Bronze leaf begonia"; robust hybrid; leaves moss-green with taffeta sheen; pink flowers. p. 38
**'Sachsen'**; angelwings dark bronzy green, underside red; free-blooming houseplant with rosy blooms. p. 33
**scabrida** (Venezuela); decorative pl. with bright green, rough-hairy leaves; small white flowers like pearls. p. 36
**sceptrum** (Brazil); large cut leaves green streaked with silver; flowers pinkish-white. p. 35

**scharffiana** (Brazil); compact, densely white-hairy species with red stems; olive fol. red beneath; pink fl.   p. 36
**scharffii** (haageana) (Brazil), "Elephant-ear begonia"; rugged, white-hairy pl. with 25 cm leaves red-veined, red beneath; large pinkish flowers with beards.   p. 34
**schmidtiana** (Brazil); reddish, hairy stems and olive green foliage, red beneath; flowers pale pink.   p. 34
**semp. albo-foliis**, "Calla-lily begonia"; succulent pl. with glossy leaves marbled white; tips glistening white; single pink flowers. A dainty beauty.   p. 35
**semperflorens fl. pl. 'Lady Frances'**, "Rose begonia"; waxy mahogany leaves; and a profusion of ruffly double pink flowers in constant bloom.   p. 26
**semperflorens 'Pink Pearl'**, a "Wax begonia"; of compact habit with fresh green fol.; single fl. bright rose. Ideal for window box or hanging pot.   p. 9, 25
**serratipetala** (New Guinea), "Pink spot angelwing"; beautiful with frilled leaves olive green, and iridescent pink spots; fl. pink; good basket plant.   p. 33
**x 'Thurstonii'**; bushy with white-haired red stems; angelwing lv. glossy bronzy green, red beneath; fl. pink. p. 37
**ulmifolia** (Colombia), "Elm-leaf begonia"; elm-like leaves rough brown-hairy; small white flowers.   p. 37
**x 'Veitch's Carmine'**; cane-stemmed with green leaves margined red; drooping red flowers.   p. 35
**venosa** (Brazil); fibrous-rooted pl. covered with white scurf; succulent leaves; flowers white.   p. 36
**versicolor** (China), the beautiful "Fairy carpet begonia"; silver, emerald-green and bronze, covered with red hairs; delicate.   p. 39
**x 'Viaudii'**; fibrous-rooted, hairy plant w. thick leaves olive green; large white fl.   p. 34
**vitifolia** (Brazil), "Grapeleaf begonia"; vigorous handsome species' with broad, gleaming green leaves; small pinkish flowers.   p. 37

**BELOPERONE** (*Acanthaceae*)
**guttata** (Mexico), "Shrimp plant"; 2-lipped white flowers, from showy reddish-brown shingled bracts. p. 64

**BERTOLONIA** (*Melastomaceae*)
**'Mosaica'** (So. America); a small "Jewel plant" with iridescent velvety green leaves banded white.   p. 121

**BIFRENARIA** (*Orchidaceae*)
**harrisoniae** (Brazil); lovely epiphyte with waxy 8 cm flowers ivory-white with purple lip.   p. 53

**BILLBERGIA** (*Bromeliaceae*)
**x 'Albertii'** (distachia x nutans), "Friendship plant"; tubular hyb. gray-scurfy; inflor. rosy w. green flowers p. 43
**x 'Fantasia'**, "Marbled rainbow plant"; colorful coppery urns variegated creamy-white and pink; rose bracts and blue flowers.   p. 43
**macrocalyx** (Brazil), "Fluted urn"; stiff green tubes with silver bands; floral bracts rosy; flowers blue   p. 43
**nutans** (Argentina), "Queen's tears"; slender silvery-bronze rosette; nodding inflorescence of rosy bracts; flowers edged violet.   p. 43
**pyramidalis concolor** (Brazil), "Summer torch"; apple green rosette with striking head with scarlet bracts and crimson flowers tipped purple; in summer.   p. 43
**pyramidalis var. pyramidalis** (Brazil), dark green vase faintly banded; scarlet fl. tipped blue, bracts red.   p. 43
**pyramidalis 'Striata'**, "Striped urn plant"; blue-green pubescent leaves, margins cream.   p. 43
**x 'Santa Barbara'**, "Banded urn plant"; colorful rosette scaly gray-green banded ivory, suffused pink. p. 43
**saundersii** (Bahia), "Rainbow plant"; attractive bronzy tubes blotched ivory and tinted pink.   (cover) p. 43

**BOUGAINVILLEA** (*Nyctaginaceae*)
**glabra** (Brazil), "Paper flower"; woody rambler with showy purplish bracts imitating flower petals.   p. 134
**'Harrisii'**, "Variegated paper-flower"; striking foliage grayish green splashed with glistening white.   p. 5, 123

**BOUVARDIA** (*Rubiaceae*)
**ternifolia 'Rosea'**, "Pink trompetilla"; shrubby, with hairy leaves, and flower clusters exquisite rose pink.   p. 65

**BOWIEA** (*Liliaceae*)
**volubilis** (So. Africa), "Climbing onion"; succulent green bulb, yearly sending up a stringy stem.   p. 134

**BRASSAIA** (*Araliaceae*)
**actinophylla** (Queensland, New Guinea), known in hort. as "Schefflera", the "Umbrella tree"; grand tub plant with glossy green, compound leaves.   p. 73

**BRASSAVOLA** (*Orchidaceae*)
**nodosa** (C. America), "Lady of the night"; charming greenish-yellow fl. with white lip, fragrant at night.   p. 53
**digbyana** (C. America); spectacular 10–15 cm flowers tinged purple; creamy lip fringed around margin.   p. 53

**BRASSIA** (*Orchidaceae*)
**gireoudiana** (C. America), a "Spider orchid"; magnificent spidery fl. yellow spotted with brown; lemon lip marked purple.   p. 53
**verrucosa** (C. America), "Queen's umbrella"; spidery, waxy flowers greenish-yellow spotted purple; brown-warty lip white.   p. 53

**BREYNIA** (*Euphorbiaceae*)
**nivosa roseo-picta** (South Seas), "Leaf-flower" or "Snow bush"; papery foliage green, white and pink, on red stems.   p. 120

**BROWALLIA** (*Solanaceae*)
**speciosa alba** (So. America), "White bush-violet"; profuse herb with large 4 cm flowers white.   p. 133

**BRUNFELSIA** (*Solanaceae*)
**latifolia** (Trop. America), "Kiss-me-quick"; shrub with fragrant 4 cm fl. pale violet, changing to white.   p. 66

**BUXUS** (*Buxaceae*)
**microphylla japonica** (Japan), "California boxwood"; dense evergreen with small 1–2 cm leathery, glossy green leaves.   p. 79

**CALADIUM** (*Araceae*)
**'Ace of Spades'**, "Lance leaf"; delicate-looking but sturdy trop. herb; marbled rose, white with red veins. p. 98
**'Candidum'**, "White fancy-leaved caladium"; glistening white leaves traced with dark green veins.   p. 98
**'Frieda Hemple'**, "Red elephant-ear"; bushy, compact and sturdy; bright red, scarlet ribs, edged green.   p. 98
**humboldtii** (argyrites) (Para), "Miniature caladium"; tiny green leaves with translucent white areas.   p. 98
**'Lord Derby'**, "Transparent caladium"; translucent, quilted leaf rose pink with green network.   p. 98

**CALANTHE** (*Orchidaceae*)
**x bella**; the Orient's "Beautiful flower"; terrestrial w. plaited leaves; handsome blooms white, pink and crimson. Largely used as cut flowers.   p. 54

**CALATHEA** (*Marantaceae*)
**argyraea** (Brazil), "Silver calathea"; feathered vein areas green, silvery between, reverse wine-red.   p. 116
**insignis** (Brazil), "Rattlesnake plant"; very pretty; yellow green with lateral ovals dark; underside maroon.   p. 117
**lietzei** (Brazil); deep green with lateral bands of silver; purple beneath.   p. 117
**louisae** (Brazil); broad leaves dark green with yellowish feathering, purple underside; flowers white.   p. 117
**makoyana** (Brazil), "Peacock plant"; fantastic, with feather design olive over translucent yellowish, purplish beneath.   p. 5, 8, 117
**micans** (Peru), "Miniature maranta"; tiny leaves to 10 cm, green with silver centerband.   p. 116
**ornata 'Roseo-lineata'** (Guyana); metallic olive-green with pairs of rosy lateral stripes.   p. 116
**picturata vandenheckei** (Amazonas); dwarf plant; deep olive with 3 bands of silver; wine-red beneath. p. 117
**picturata 'Wendlingeri'** ('Argentea') (Venezuela); entire leaf shining silver, green border, red beneath.   p. 117
**roseo-picta** (Brazil); rounded 20 cm leaf olive green w. red midrib, outer zone of silver; underside purple. p. 116
**undulata** (Peru); dark green with jagged band of greenish silver, purple beneath.   p. 116
**veitchiana** (Ecuador); striking, with peacock-feather in shades of green, brown and bluish.   p. 117
**zebrina** (Brazil), "Zebra plant"; magnificent to 1 m tall; deep velvety green w. pale ribs; purple beneath.   p. 9, 117

**CALCEOLARIA** (*Scrophulariaceae*)
**herbeohybrida 'Multiflora nana'**, "Lady's pocketbook"; clusters of pouch-flowers in shades of orange, tigered red.   p. 24

**CALLISIA** (*Commelinaceae*)
**elegans** (Mexico), "Striped inch plant"; succulent green leaves striped white; purple beneath.   p. 130
**fragrans** (Tradescantia dracaenoides) (Mexico); fleshy rosette sending out runners; glossy green.   p. 130
**fragrans 'Melnikoff'** (Spironema in hort.); fleshy, glossy green leaves banded with yellow, to 20 cm.   p. 131

**CALLISTEMON** (*Myrtaceae*)
**lanceolatus** (Australia), "Crimson bottle-brush"; shrub with silky twigs, cylindric spikes of crimson stamens.   p. 67

**CALLOPSIS** (*Araceae*)
**volkensis** (Tanzania), "Miniature calla"; only 10 cm high; cupped spathe waxy-white.   p. 96

**CAMELLIA** (*Theaceae*)
**japonica 'Elegans'** (Japan), "Peony camellia"; glossy foliage; 10 cm flowers carmine, variegated white.   p. 66

**CAMPANULA** (*Campanulaceae*)
**isophylla mayii,** "Italian bellflower"; herbaceous basket plant; pale blue 4 cm flowers.                      p. 133
**CAMPELIA**
**zanonia 'Mexican Flag',** (Dichorisandra albo-lineata); l. green leaves to 30 cm, banded white, edged red. p. 9, 131
**CAPSICUM** (*Solanaceae*)
**annuum 'Birdseye',** "Christmas pepper"; fresh green leaves on dense bush; numerous white flowers followed by waxy, 1 cm scarlet berries in winter.                      p. 69
**CARALLUMA** (*Asclepiadaceae*)
**nebrownii** (S.W. Africa), "Spiked clubs"; fat 4-angled stems gray-green, marbled red; starflowers brown.    p. 151
**CAREX** (*Cyperaceae*)
**foliosissima albo-mediana** (Japan), "Miniature variegated sedge"; grass-like tufts; green, white stripes.      p. 86
**CARISSA** (*Apocynaceae*)
**acokanthera** (So. Africa), "Bushman's poison"; glossy foliage, and very fragrant white flowers; poisonous black fruit and sap.                                              p. 66
**grandiflora** (So. Africa), "Natal plum"; spiny shrub; fragrant white flowers; plum-like red fruit.         p. 71
**CARLUDOVICA** (*Cyclanthaceae*)
**palmata** (Ecuador north), "Panama hat plant"; palm-like fan-leaves cut into 4 divisions.                   p. 100
**CARYOTA** (*Palmae*)
**mitis** (Burma south), "Dwarf fishtail palm"; clustering palm; leaves with pinnae fan-shaped.              p. 99
**CATASETUM** (*Orchidaceae*)
**saccatum christyanum** (Amazon); epiphyte with fragrant 10 cm fl. brown; green lip marked purple.       p. 54
**CATHARANTHUS** (*Apocynaceae*)
**roseus** (**Vinca rosea** in hort.) (Pantropic), "Madagascar periwinkle"; leaves with white rib; 4 cm flowers usually rosy-red with purple throat; showy in hot summer.    p. 31
**CATTLEYA** (*Orchidaceae*)
**bowringiana** (Honduras), "Cluster cattleya"; prolific with firm 8 cm rosy flowers, lip with maroon.       p. 55
**dowiana aurea** (Colombia),,"Queen cattleya"; beautiful, fragrant 15 cm fl. golden-yellow with crimson lip. p. 55
**forbesii** (So. Brazil), a "Cocktail orchid"; waxy, fragrant flowers yellow green, lip streaked with red.      p. 55
**intermedia alba** (Brazil), another "Cocktail orchid"; heavy-textured, fragrant white flowers with crisped lip p. 55
**lueddemanniana** (Venezuela); handsome epiphyte with 15 cm rosy flowers; lip purple.                      p. 55
**mossiae** (Venezuela), "Easter orchid"; magnificent 12–15 cm fragrant fl. blush rose, frilled lip crimson.  p. 55
**skinneri** (Guatemala); clusters of 5–8 cm flowers with rosy sepals and petals and dark lip.               p. 55
**trianaei** (Colombia), "Christmas orchid"; lovely winter bloomer; sepals and petals rose, lip crimson.     p. 55
**CEDRUS** (*Pinaceae*)
**atlantica glauca** (Algeria), "Blue Atlas cedar"; tufted needles silvery-blue; majestic tub conifer.         p. 104
**CEPHALOCEREUS** (*Cactaceae*)
**senilis** (Mexico), "Old man cactus"; grayish column covered by long silver-white hairs.               p. 9, 136
**CERATOPTERIS** (*Filices*)
**thalictroides** (Pan-tropic), "Water fern", for aquaria; bizarre light green succulent fronds.             p. 112
**CEREUS** (*Cactaceae*)
**hexagonus** (Colombia), "South American blue column"; glaucous-blue-green, large white flowers.          p. 137
**"peruvianus"** hort., "Column-cactus"; the commonly cultivated tree-cereus; handsome fleshy, bluish green columns with few spines; whitish blooms.        p. 9, 137
**peruvianus monstrosus,** the "Curiosity plant"; freakish form with many heads, brown spines.              p. 72
**CEROPEGIA** (*Asclepiadaceae*)
**woodii** (Rhodesia), "String of hearts"; charming 2 cm bluish leaves marbled silver, on purplish threads. p. 133
**CESTRUM** (*Solanaceae*)
**nocturnum** (W. Indies), "Night jessamine"; 2 cm flowers powerfully perfumed at night.                     p. 64
**CHAMAECEREUS** (*Cactaceae*)
**silvestri** (Argentina), "Peanut-cactus"; miniature clustered fingers with white bristles; flowers orange-scarlet. p. 142
**CHAMAEDOREA** (*Palmae*)
**elegans** (Mexico), "Parlor palm"; small and graceful, cluster-forming; excellent keeper.               p. 13, 100
**erumpens** (Honduras), "Bamboo palm"; suckering, with slender canes and dark leaves, a decorator's favorite. With oriental grace; good keeper.              p. 13, 100
**metallica** (tenella in hort.) (Mexico), "Miniature fishtail"; curious with broad leaves forked; to 1 m high.  p. 100

**CHAMAERANTHEMUM** (*Acanthaceae*)
**gaudichaudii** (Brazil); low creeper w. 5–8 cm leaves painted silver.                                        p. 122
**igneum** (Peru); beautiful veloured, brownish leaves with red to yellow pattern.                          p. 5, 114
**venosum** (Brazil); low plant w. 8–10 cm grayish leaves netted w. silver.                                   p. 122
**CHAMAEROPS** (*Palmae*)
**humilis** (Spain, Morocco), "European fan palm"; usually dwarf; tough dull green fans.                     p. 102
**CHIRITA** (*Gesneriaceae*)
**lavandulacea** (Malaya), "Hindustan gentian"; soft-hairy light green leaves; 2–3 cm flowers pale lavender. p. 50
**CHLOROPHYTUM** (*Liliaceae*)
**bichetii** (W. Africa), "St. Bernard's lily"; pretty with leaves fresh green striped white.                  p. 82
**comosum 'Variegatum'** (So. Africa), "Large spider plant" or "Green-lily"; fresh green leaves to 3 cm wide, edged in white.                                      p. 82
**comosum 'Vittatum'** (Cape Prov.), "Spider plant"; narrow-leaved w. white center band; plantlets develop on floral stalk.                                       p. 82
**CHORIZEMA** (*Leguminosae*)
**cordatum** (W. Australia), "Australian flame pea"; shrub w. tiny toothed 3–5 cm leaves; flowers orange with yellow. Miniature house plant for hanging baskets.  p. 67
**CHRYSALIDOCARPUS** (*Palmae*)
**lutescens** (Madagascar), "Areca palm"; graceful, clustering w. slender yell. stems; yell.-gr. pinnae.   p. 101
**CHRYSANTHEMUM** (*Compositae*)
**frutescens** (Canary Isl.), "White Marguerite" or "Paris daisy"; herbaceous green, lacy foliage; white flowers with yellow disk.                                      p. 26
**morifolium 'Golden Lace',** "Spider mum" or "Fuji mum"; threadlike, yellow tubular florets.           p. 26
**morifolium 'Princess Ann';** an excellent "Pot mum"; long-lasting "decorative" peach pink flowers.        p. 26
**morifolium 'Yellow Delaware',** a semi-incurved "Mum plant"; rich yellow flowers (Nov.)             p. 15
**CHYSIS** (*Orchidaceae*)
**aurea** (Mexico to Peru); deciduous epiphyte; waxy aromatic 5–8 cm fl., reddish with yellow.            p. 53
**CIBOTIUM** (*Filices*)
**chamissoi,** known as "Menziesii" in Hawaii, the "Man tree fern"; trunk with brown hairs; fronds nile-green, leathery; will grow in water.                      p. 105
**schiedei** (So. Mexico), "Mexican treefern"; good decorator plant with graceful, durable fronds light green Dainty-looking, yet good keeper indoors.        p. 105
**CISSUS** (*Vitaceae*)
**adenopoda** (Tanzania), "Pink cissus"; coppery leaves covered w. purple hair, red beneath.            p. 128
**antarctica** (New South Wales), "Kangaroo vine"; leaves to 15 cm, metallic green; excell. indoors. p. 9, 128
**discolor** (Java), "Rex begonia vine"; beautiful tendril-climber; green, silver and purple; reverse maroon.  p. 128
**rhombifolia,** in hort. as "Vitis" or "Rhoicissus" (W. Indies), "Grape-ivy"; one of the best indoor ramblers with metallic green foliage.                          p. 128
**rhombifolia 'Mandaiana',** "Bold grape-ivy"; tendril vine with larger, firm leaves shining like wax.       p. 128
**rotundifolia** (E. Africa), "Arabian wax cissus"; waxy-fleshy 6–8 cm leaves glossy green.              p. 128
**CITRUS** (*Rutaceae*)
**aurantium** (Vietnam), "Sour Seville orange"; fragrant, white-waxy flowers; with age large orange fruit; the tub orange of the Middle Ages.                        p. 70
**aurantium myrtifolia** (China), "Myrtleleaf orange"; small, stiff 3 cm leaves, fragrant white fl., and small, sour fruits. Excellent as container plant.             p. 70
**limon 'Ponderosa'** (Maryland hyb.), "American wonder-lemon"; popular in tubs; big 12 cm fruit weighing 1 kg., with sour juice.                                  p. 70
**x 'Meyeri',** "Dwarf Chinese lemon" or "Meyer lemon"; sweet-scented white fl.; good quality lemons at early stage. A conversation plant, easily grown in pots.       p. 70
**mitis** (China), "Calamondin orange"; miniature mandarin; fragrant fl.; small 2–4 cm fruits easily produced. p. 69
**paradisi** (W. Indies), "Grapefruit"; large white flowers; heavy 10–12 cm fruit; used in tubs.             p. 70
**taitensis** (South Pacific), "Otaheite orange"; dwarf ornamental for pots; waxy-white fl.; golden 4–5 cm fruit w. tart juice.                                       p. 69
**CLEISTOCACTUS** (*Cactaceae*)
**smaragdiflorus** (Argentina), "Firecracker-cactus"; slender 5 cm stems w. yellow spines; scarlet flowers. p. 142

**straussii** (Bolivia), the lovely "Silver torch"; slender white-bristled columns; flowers red. p. 136

**CLERODENDRUM** (*Verbenaceae*)

**x speciosum,** "Glory-bower"; scandent branches w. glossy leaves; clusters of crimson flowers. p. 68

**CLIVIA** (*Amaryllidaceae*)

**miniata 'Grandiflora'** (Natal), "Scarlet kafir lily"; from dark leathery leaves rises a cluster of flaming-scarlet erect, lily-like flowers with yellow throat. p. 28

**CLUSIA** (*Guttiferae*)

**rosea** (W. Indies), "Autograph tree" or "Fat pork tree"; durable thick-leathery, deep green leaves to 20 cm. p. 83

**COCCOLOBA** (*Polygonaceae*)

**uvifera** (W. Indies), "Sea-grape"; decorative shrub w. stiff-leathery 20 cm leaves, glossy olive w. red veins. p. 83

**COCCOTHRINAX** (*Palmae*)

**argentata** (Bahamas, Florida), "Florida silver palm"; small star-shaped leaves glossy green, silver beneath. p. 102

**CODIAEUM** (*Euphorbiaceae*)

**'Aucubaefolium'** (Polynesian), "Aucuba-leaf croton"; bushy w. small glossy green leaves spotted yellow. p. 118

**'Duke of Windsor';** robust croton always colorful; green and orange w. red midrib. p. 5

**'Elaine',** "Lance-leaf croton"; stiff leaves fresh green w. yellow veins tinted pink. p. 118

**'Gloriosum superbum',** "Autumn croton"; large foliage green, yell. veins, maturing to red with crimson. p. 118

**'Imperialis',** "Appleleaf croton"; handsome with 12 cm leaves yellow, shading to peach and red. p. 118

**'Johanna Coppinger',** "Strap-leaf croton"; dark green variegated yellow to orange, ribs red. p. 118

**'L.M. Rutherford',** "Giant croton"; showy plant with foliage pink with gold and crimson on green. p. 118

**'Mona Lisa',** "White croton"; outstanding creamy-white, edged green, later tinted red. p. 118

**'Norwood Beauty',** "Oakleaf-croton"; smallish, with tough 15 cm lv. dark green with brown, yellow. p. 118

**'Punctatum aureum',** "Miniature croton"; bushy with linear fol. glossy green spotted yellow. p. 118

**COELOGYNE** (*Orchidaceae*)

**cristata** (Nepal); easy-growing epiphyte with large 8–12 cm fragrant flowers glistening white. p. 54

**dayana** (Malaysia), "Neck-lace orchid"; striking lemon and chocolate 6 cm flowers, pendulous chainlike. p. 54

**lawrenceana** (Vietnam); small epiphyte with showy 10 cm waxy fl. buff-yellow, lip white and brown. p. 54

**sparsa** (Philippines); dwarf epiphyte with small 3 cm fragrant fl. white tinted green; lip dotted purple. p. 54

**COFFEA** (*Rubiaceae*)

**arabica** (Ethiopia), "Arabian coffee tree"; handsome with lustrous leaves; fragrant white fl.; crimson berries containing 2 beans. p. 71

**COLEUS** (*Labiatae*)

**blumei 'Defiance'** (Java), a "Painted nettle"; herbaceous foliage brownish red bordered with broad yellow margin. Long used in bedding planting. p. 30

**rehneltianus 'Trailing Queen'** (Ceylon), a colorful "Trailing coleus" with 3–5 cm leaves purple with red, bordered in shades of green. p. 132

**COLOCASIA** (*Araceae*)

**antiquorum illustris** (E. Indies), "Black caladium"; soft leaves green in vein areas, balance black-purple. p. 97

**COLUMNEA** (*Gesneriacea*)

**linearis** (Costa Rica); attractive "Goldfish plant" with axillary 4 cm flowers silky rose-pink; for baskets. p. 49

**microphylla** (Costa Rica), "Small-leaved goldfish vine"; pendant branches with hairy 1 cm leaves; 2-lipped 6–8 cm flowers scarlet with yellow patch on bottom. p. 49

**verecunda** (Costa Rica); erect plant with waxy leaves; axillary flared yellow flowers, wine-colored underneath. p. 49

**CORDYLINE** (*Liliaceae*)

**australis** (New Zealand), in hort. as "Dracaena indivisa", the "Cabbage tree"; juvenile leaves narrow linear. p. 85

**indivisa 'Rubra'** (New Zealand), "Red palm-lily"; broadleaved with flexible-leathery foliage dark bronze; fragrant white flowers. p. 85

**stricta** (Dracaena congesta in hort.), (Eastern Australia); sword-shaped leathery leaves matte green or reddish with rough edges. p. 81

**terminalis 'Baby Ti'** (Hawaii); miniature rosette of narrow, recurved coppery leaves bordered red. p. 5

**terminalis 'Negri',** the "Black dracaena"; big leathery, glossy copper-maroon leaves almost black. p. 85

**terminalis var. 'Ti'** (South Pacific), "Good luck plant" or "Miracle plant"; leaves plain green. Cane sections will sprout young plants. p. 81

**terminalis 'Trioclor',** "Tricolored dracaena"; colorful rosette of broad leaves red, pink, cream over green. p. 81

**COSTUS** (*Zingiberaceae*)

**malortieanus** (Costa Rica), "Emerald spiral ginger"; fleshy emerald green, silky leaves arranged in spiral around stem; flowers yellow, marked brown-red. p. 84

**sanguineus** (C. America), beautiful "Spiral flag"; spiralling leaves bluish velvet with silver band; blood-red beneath. p. 5

**COTYLEDON** (*Crassulaceae*)

**barbeyi** (Arabia), "Hoary navelwort"; shovel-shaped thick leaves hoary white. p. 146

**undulata** (So. Africa), "Silver crown"; beautiful with thick wedge-shaped leaves silver gray; apex crimped. p. 9

**CRASSULA** (*Crassulaceae*)

**arborescens** ("argentea" in hort.) (So. Africa), "Silver dollar"; handsome succulent with thick leaves silver-gray and red margin. p. 147

**argentea** ("arborescens" in hort., bot. obliqua), the "Jade plant"; thick fleshy 3–5 cm leaves glossy bright green, edged red; small pinkish-white starry flowers. Favorite disgarden plant. p. 147

**cultrata** (So. Africa), "Propeller plant"; light green succulent leaves twisted in opposite directions. p. 145

**dubia;** "obvallata" in hort. (So. Africa); leaves arranged diagonally, white-felted, gray-green w. red edge. p. 147

**lactea** (Natal), "Tailor's patch"; flat, smooth leaves green with sunken white dots along margins. p. 145

**perforata 'Pagoda',** "Pagoda plant"; wiry stems with triangular 3–4 cm rich green leaves, fringed with hairs. p. 145

**perfossa** (So. Africa), "String o'buttons"; thin woody stem threaded with pairs of bluish leaves edged red. p. 145

**pseudolycopodioides** (S.W. Africa), "Princess pine"; small succulent, lycopodium-like, with 4-ranked scale-leaves rich green. p. 145

**rupestris** (So. Africa), "Rosary vine"; pretty with wiry stems set with 2 cm triangular gray leaves, edged red. Clusters of yellowish flowers. p. 9, 145, 147

**tetragona** (So. Africa), "Miniature pine tree"; erect stems with opposite spindle-shaped glossy green 3–4 cm leaves. Small white flowers. p. 145

**'Tricolor Jade'** (argentea x lactea), "Tricolored jade plant"; beautiful succulent variegated green, gray, white and pink. p. 9, 147

**CRINUM** (*Amaryllidaceae*)

**x powellii,** "Swamp lily"; spectacular bulbous plant with 10 cm flowers deep rose. p. 27

**CROCUS** (*Iridaceae*)

**'Vernus hybrid',** "Alpine spring crocus"; cormous herb with lilac or white fl. in early spring. p. 27

**CROSSANDRA** (*Acanthaceae*)

**infundibuliformis** (India), "Firecracker flower"; herbaceous tropical with glossy dark green 8–12 cm leaves; free-flowering salmon red. p. 64

**pungens** (Tanzania); attractive with leaves olive, in contrast with creamy veins; flowers light orange. p. 114

**CRYPTANTHUS** (*Bromeliaceae*)

**acaulis** (Brazil), "Green earth star"; small flattened rosette 10–15 cm across, green with gray scurf. p. 44

**acaulis ruber** (Brazil), "Miniature red earth star"; small rosette with leaves bronze covered by beige scurf. p. 44

**beuckeri** (Brazil), "Marbled spoon"; rosette of spoon-shaped leaves prettily painted dark over pale green. p. 45

**bivittatus lueddemannii** (Brazil), "Large rose-stripe star"; big 25–35 cm rosette; thick leaves with two pale bands over copper. p. 44

**bivittatus minor** (roseus pictus in hort.) (Brazil), "Dwarf rose-stripe star"; star-like terrestrial, coppery red with two pale bands. p. 44

**bromelioides tricolor,** "Rainbow star"; striking variegated cultivar fresh green to bronzy, banded ivory. Margins and base tinted rose in good light. p. 5, 45

**diversifolius** (Brazil), "Vary-leaf star"; rosette of leathery leaves 25 cm long, green and covered by silver scurf. p. 45

**fosterianus** (Brazil), "Stiff pheasant-leaf"; large rosette of stiff, thick leaves brown with tan zebra bands. p. 45

**x 'It'** (Foster), the spectacular "Color-band"; mutant coppery with striping of ivory; margins rosy-red. p. 45

**lacerdae** (Brazil), "Silver star"; rosette of emerald-green leaves with silver borders and pale center. p. 44

**x osyanus,** "Mottled earth-star"; irregular rosette warm-green with pale mottling, tinted pink; white fl. p. 44

**x rubescens,** "Brown earth star"; leathery leaves purplish brown with silver scales; fl. white. p. 44

**zonatus** (Brazil), "Zebra plant"; spectacular rosette 20–45 cm across, copper with tan crossbands. p. 45

**zonatus zebrinus,** "Pheasant leaf"; strikingly beautiful form with bronze-purple wavy leaves and silvery cross banding; translucent white flowers. cover, p. 9, 45

**CTENANTHE** (*Marantaceae*)

**lubbersiana** (Brazil); forking stems with leaves green, variegated yellow. p. 116

**oppenheimiana tricolor** (Brazil), "Never-never plant"; colorful tropical, highly variegated white over green and silver, underside wine-red. p. 117

**pilosa** (compressa) (Brazil), in hort. as "Bamburanta"; sturdy foliage plant with leathery, waxy green leaves. p. 116

**CUPHEA** (*Lythraceae*)

**hyssopifolia** (Guatemala), "False heather"; woody shrublet w. tiny needles, small starry purplish flowers. p. 78

**platycentra** (Mexico), "Cigar flower"; attractive window plant, with scarlet flowers tipped white and black. p. 68

**CURCULIGO** (*Amaryllidaceae*)

**capitulata** (Java), "Palm grass"; tropical foliage plant w. plaited leaves glossy green to 1 m long. p. 100

**CYANOTIS** (*Commelinaceae*)

**kewensis** (India), "Teddy-bear vine"; succulent, dense with 3 cm olive gr., br.-woolly leaves, violet beneath. p. 130

**somaliensis** (E. Africa), "Pussy-ears"; glossy green fleshy 4 cm leaves covered with white hair; fl. blue. p. 130

**CYATHEA** (*Filices*)

**arborea** (Puerto Rico), "West Indian treefern"; graceful with slender trunk to 16 m; crown of fresh green fronds. p. 4

**CYCAS** (*Cycadaceae*)

**circinalis** (So. India to Philippines), "Fern palm"; graceful rosette of glossy dark green fronds; good tub plant. p. 100

**revoluta** (So. Japan), "Sago palm"; hulking trunk topped by crown of stiff-leathery, glossy fronds. p. 100

**CYCLAMEN** (*Primulaceae*)

**persicum 'Perle von Zehlendorf',** "Florists cyclamen" or "Alpine violet"; cherished winter-bloomer with leaves patterned silver; flowers deep salmon from basal tuber. p. 23

**CYCLANTHUS** (*Cyclanthaceae*)

**bipartitus** (Guyana), "Splitleaf cyclanthus"; decorative leathery, quilted leaves with milky juice, forked at apex. Scented flowers aroid-like, with yellow spathe. p. 100

**CYCNOCHES** (*Orchidaceae*)

**egertonianum** (Mexico to Brazil); beautiful epiphyte with different male and female flowers, greenish suffused with purple. p. 54

**CYMBALARIA** (*Scrophulariaceae*)

**muralis** (So. Europe to W. Asia), "Kenilworth ivy"; herb with thread-like stems, fresh green, waxy leaves, tiny lilac blue flowers with yellow throat; for baskets. p. 132

**CYMBIDIUM** (*Orchidaceae*)

**x alexanderi,** a "Corsage cymbidium"; robust terrestrial with waxy, long-lasting 10–12 cm fl. white flushed pink; usually blooming in spring. p. 54

**'Flirtation',** "Miniature hybrid cymbidium"; exquisite pot plant with 5 cm durable flowers, pink to greenish ivory and purple. p. 54

**CYPERUS** (*Cyperaceae*)

**alternifolius** (Madagascar), "Umbrella plant"; bogplant with stalks bearing crown of green, grass-like leaves. p. 86

**CYRTOMIUM** (*Filices*)

**falcatum** (Japan to India), "Fishtail fern"; handsome leathery fronds shining dark green; very durable. p. 106

**falc. 'Rochfordianum',** the popular "Holly fern"; robust with broader, glossy fronds wavy at margins, tolerant of neglect. p. 106

**DARLINGTONIA** (*Sarraceniaceae*)

**californica** (California, Oregon), "Cobra plant" or "California pitcher plant"; insectivorous bogplant, yellowish with purple; entraps insects. p. 120

**DASYLIRION** (*Liliaceae*)

**acrotriche** (Mexico), "Bear-grass"; dense rosette of narrow, spine-tipped leaves 4 cm wide. p. 85

**DATURA** (*Solanaceae*)

**suaveolens** (So. Brazil), "Angel's trumpet"; tall shrub with large leaves and pendulous 30 cm fragrant flowers white; blooming mainly late summer. p. 65

**DAVALLIA** (*Filices*)

**bullata mariesii** (Japan), "Ball fern"; hairy rhizomes with small 15 cm lacy fronds, very durable. p. 108

**fejeensis** (Fiji Islands), "Rabbit's-foot fern"; brown-woolly, creeping rhizomes with lacy but coarse, firm fronds. Excellent for hanging baskets. p. 108

**fejeensis plumosa** (Polynesia), "Dainty rabbit's-foot"; dwarf variety with fresh green fronds finely divided. p. 108

**trichomanoides** (Malaya), "Carrot fern"; robust epiphyte with 20 cm leathery fronds coarsely cut. p. 108

**DENDROBIUM** (*Orchidaceae*)

**aggregatum** (So. China); charming epiphyte with 4 cm flowers golden yellow with orange. p. 57

**densiflorum** (Assam); sturdy canes with beautiful 4 cm flowers sparkling golden yellow with velvety orange-yellow lip, in dense trusses. p. 57

**falconeri** (Burma); profuse epiphyte with fragrant 10 cm white flowers tipped purple, lip orange. p. 57

**johnsoniae** (New Guinea); noble epiphyte with large 10–12 cm white flowers; lip purple inside. p. 57

**moschatum** (Himalayas); handsome with tall canes bearing lovely 8–10 cm heavy textured fl. yellow tipped with rose; purple eyes. p. 57

**nobile** (Himalayas to Taiwan); free-blooming with large fragrant 8 cm white fl. tipped rose; crimson throat. p. 57

**phalaenopsis** (Queensland to Timor); beautiful with arching sprays of 8 cm fl.; sepals magenta, petals rose, lip dark red. p. 57

**primulinum** (Burma); free-blooming with fragrant 6 cm rosy flowers with yellow lip streaked red. p. 57

**thyrsiflorum** (Himalayas); showy epiphyte with fragrant 5 cm flowers white, the lip orange, in heavy sprays. p. 57

**DENDROCHILUM** (*Orchidaceae*)

**glumaceum** (syn. Platyclinis), a popular "Chain orchid"; arching slender 30 cm spikes of scented straw-white flowers, easily grown. p. 58

**DIASTEMA** (*Gesneriaceae*)

**quinquevulnerum** (Colombia); stiff-hairy plant with bright green leaves; dainty tubular 2 cm white flowers, the lobes each with a purple spot. p. 50

**DICHORISANDRA** (*Commelinaceae*)

**reginae** (Peru), "Queen's spiderwort"; beautiful with 15 cm leaves banded and spotted silver, center metallic violet; flowers lavender. p. 131

**thyrsiflora** (Brazil), the "Blue ginger"; stout canes bear rosettes of glossy green leaves, topped by showy deep blue flowers with yellow anthers. p. 130

**thyrsiflora variegata;** attractive variety with 15 cm leaves having 2 silver bands alongside red midrib. p. 131

**DICKSONIA** (*Filices*)

**squarrosa** (New Zealand), "Rough New Zealand treefern"; black trunk bears crown of horizontal, leathery fronds dark green, harsh to the touch. p. 105

**DIEFFENBACHIA** (*Araceae*)

**amoena** (Colombia), "Giant dumbcane"; sturdy and handsome with glossy green 30–45 cm leaves feathered with cream. Excellent decorative table plant. p. 95

**x bausei;** compact plant featuring beautiful leaves yellowish with dark green and white spots. p. 95

**'Exotica'** ('Arvida') (Costa Rica); shapely and compact with firm leaves deep matte-green and richly splashed with cream, and of good texture. p. 5

**leoniae** (Colombia); handsome plant with satiny, firm foliage friendly green with dominant yellow variegation. Very attractive but requires warmth. p. 95

**picta** (Brazil: Amazonas), "Spotted dumbcane"; popular, handsome house plant with glossy green leaves and ivory blotching, to 25 cm long. p. 9, 95

**picta 'Rud. Roehrs'** (Roehrs 1937), "Gold dieffenbachia"; striking mutant with colorful leaves almost entirely yellow or chartreuse, midrib and border dark green; excellent house plant, thrives in dry-warm room. p. 9, 95

**picta 'Superba',** in hort. as "Roehrs superba"; attractive, compact mutant with durable, thicker foliage highly variegated white over glossy green. p. 95

**DIMORPHOTHECA** (*Compositae*)

**ecklonis** (So. Africa), "Cape marigold"; large daisy-like 8 cm flowers with ray-florets white above, purplish beneath, and blue center disk. p. 62

**DINTERANTHUS** (*Aizoaceae*)

**wilmotianus** (So. Africa), "Split rock"; tiny succulent of 2 cm dia., with paired fat leaves, grayish with violet dots; flowers golden-yellow. Keep dry when resting. p. 146

**DIONAEA**

**muscipula** (No. and So. Carolina), the popular "Venus fly-trap"; small carnivorous plant, with traps of leaf pairs yellowish green, and red inside. p. 120

**DIOSCOREA** (*Dioscoreaceae*)

**bulbifera** (Philippines), "Air-potato" or "True yam"; odd twiner forming brown aerial tubers to 30 cm long. p. 134

**DIPLADENIA** (*Apocynaceae*)

**sanderi** (Brazil), "Rose dipladenia"; woody vine w. milky sap; beautiful 6–8 cm flowers rose pink w. yellow throat; blooming throughout the year. p. 134

**DIZYGOTHECA** '(*Araliaceae*)
   **elegantissima** (New Hebrides), "Spider aralia"; graceful tropical shrub with flexuous, mottled stems and leathery leaves with threadlike segments metallic brown.          p. 74
**DRACAENA** (*Liliaceae*)
   **arborea** (W. Africa), "Tree dracaena"; trunk with dense head of sword-shaped fresh green leaves.          p. 81
   **deremensis 'Warneckei'** (Trop. Africa), "Striped dracaena"; handsome and durable, symmetrical rosette of sword-shaped green leaves (to 40 cm) banded white. Good decorative plant even in poor light.          p. 4, 14, 80
   **draco** (Canary Islands), "Dragon tree"; decorative rosette of crowded, thick-fleshy leaves bluish green.          p. 81
   **fragrans massangeana** (West Africa), "Cornstalk plant"; old-fashioned houseplant with broad and arching, rich green leaves, banded yellow in center.          p. 13, 80
   **fragrans 'Victoriae'**, "Painted dragon-lily"; stunningly beautiful but delicate; green foliage bordered by broad margins of cream.          p. 80
   **godseffiana** (Africa: Zaïre), "Gold-dust dracaena"; charming small plant with leaves glossy green spotted cream. Much used in terrariums.          p. 9, 80
   **godseffiana 'Florida Beauty';** striking seedling cultivar with leathery leaves richly variegated cream; excellent for dishgardens.          p. 80
   **goldieana** (So. Nigeria), "Queen of dracaenas"; spectacular but difficult, with broad foliage deep green, strikingly marked with cross bands of near white.          p. 3, 80
   **hookeriana** (Natal), "Leather dracaena"; heavy plant with thick leaves dark green and glossy, to 5 cm wide; tough as leather.          p. 81
   **marginata** (Madagascar), "Madagascar dragon tree"; favorite decorator, artistic with slender snaky stems and narrow leathery, dark, 40 cm leaves edged red; very durable. Tolerant to poor light to 30 ft-candles.          p. 9, 13, 81
   **sanderiana** (Cameroons), "Ribbon plant"; durable little rosette of leathery 15–20 cm green leaves with broad white marginal bands; for dishgardens or water culture. p. 3, 5, 80
**DRIMIOPSIS** (*Liliaceae*)
   **kirkii** (Zanzibar); small bulbous plant with fleshy leaves blue-green with dark blotches; flowers white.          p. 122
**DYCKIA** (*Bromeliaceae*)
   **brevifolia** (So. Brazil), "Miniature agave"; succulent rosette of glossy green sharp-pointed leaves; flowers bright orange.          p. 44
   **fosteriana** (Paraná), "Silver and gold dyckia"; spreading rosette of stiff silvery 20 cm leaves, margins with silver spines; floral spike of orange flowers.          p. 44
**ECHEVERIA** (*Crassulaceae*)
   **derenbergii** (Oaxaca), "Painted lady"; miniature succulent 4–6 cm globe waxy silvery-blue, tipped red; charming for dishgardens.          p. 147
   **elegans** (Mexico), "Mexican snowball"; exquisite incurved rosette 5–10 cm dia. waxy pale blue; coral pink flowers. Excellent for dish gardens and small pots. p. 147
   **gilva** (Mexico), "Wax rosette"; durable open rosette. pea green and slightly glaucous, tip flushed orange red. Very attractive in dishgardens.          p. 148
   **glauca** (Mexico), "Blue echeveria"; open rosette 10 cm across; leaves glaucous gray-green tipped with red; flowers red and yellow.          p. 9, 148
   **multicaulis** (Guerrero), "Copper rose"; branching stems each with small rosette of waxy coppery leaves 3–4 cm long. Red flowers, yellowish inside.          p. 146
   **peacockii var. subsessilis,** desmetiana hort. (Mexico); beautiful rosette covered with waxy bluish-white bloom, margins red; red flowers.          p. 148
   **'Pulv-oliver',** "Plush plant"; fine plushy hybrid with leaves edged maroon toward apex, covered with glistening white hairs.          p. 147
   **'Set-oliver',** "Maroon chenille plant"; plush-covered olive green leaves, edged maroon; fl. yellow to red.     p. 9
**ECHINOCACTUS** (*Cactaceae*)
   **grusonii** (C. Mexico), "Golden barrel"; striking globe to 1 m dia., light green and covered with yellow spines. Yellow flowers imbedded around top.          p. 139
**ECHINOCEREUS** (*Cactaceae*)
   **dasyacanthus** (W. Texas), "Rainbow cactus"; cylindric to 20 cm high, the stiff spines attractive with zones of yellow, purple, amethyst; fl. yellow.          p. 9
   **purpureus** (Oklahoma), "Purple hedgehog"; cylindric to 12 cm high, olive green covered with white radial spines tipped purple; flowers deep magenta purple.          p. 136
**ECHINOPSIS** (*Cactaceae*)
   **multiplex** (So. Brazil), "Easter-lily cactus"; small barrel to 15 cm high, forming clusters; green w. brown spines; showy rosy, fragrant flowers.          p. 136

**EPIDENDRUM** (*Orchidaceae*)
   **atropurpureum** (W. Indies to Peru), "Spice orchid"; lovely heavy-textured, fragrant 5–8 cm flowers chocolate with green, lip white with crimson.          p. 56
   **brassavolae** (Mexico to Panama); graceful with waxy, spidery, sweet-scented flowers yellowish brown, lip white with purple.          p. 56
   **cochleatum** (Cuba to Brazil), "Cockle-shelled orchid"; curious upside-down flowers greenish-white, lip violet with yellow, long-lived.          p. 56
   **ibaguense** (radicans in hort.), "Fiery reed orchid"; handsome terrestrial; long reed-stems with waxy orange-scarlet 3 cm flowers; easy to grow.          p. 56
   **mariae** (So. Mexico); lovely little epiphyte with waxy 8 cm flowers greenish-yellow with white lip.          p. 56
   **pentotis** (C. America); compact epiphyte with waxy, fragrant flowers greenish-white, lip white with purple. p. 56
   **prismatocarpum** (Costa Rica), the beautiful "Rainbow orchid"; fragrant, waxy 5 cm flowers yellow blotched maroon, lip rosy red.          p. 56
   **radiatum** (Costa Rica); compact plant with fleshy cream-white blossoms, lip with purple lines.          p. 56
   **stamfordianum** (Panama); beautiful with fragrant 3–4 cm flowers yellow, spotted with red.          p. 56
**x EPIPHRONITIS** (*Orchidaceae*)
   **veitchii** (Epidendrum x Sophronitis); reedstems topped by fiery red 3 cm flowers yellow on lip.          p. 58
**EPIPHYLLUM** (*Cactaceae*)
   **x hybridus,** a typical "Orchid cactus"; large flowers in iridescent colors nearly blue, to red, pink and white.   p. 141
   **hybrid 'Elegantissimum',** a superb basket type of "Dwarf orchid cactus"; showy with large perfect bright crimson flowers.          p. 141
   **oxypetalum** (Mexico), "Queen of the night"; night-blooming with large fragrant white flowers.          p. 141
**EPIPREMNUM** (*Araceae*)
   **pinnatum** (Malaysia), "Taro vine"; tropical climber with glossy green leaves, pinholes as silvery dots along midrib. The Asiatic parallel to Monsteras or Philodendrons. p. 97
**EPISCIA** (*Gesneriaceae*)
   **cupreata 'Acajou';** exquisite quilted 8–10 cm leaves mahogany with silver; orange-red flowers.          p. 9, 50
   **cupreata 'Frosty';** lustrous with downy emerald-green leaves with silver; flowers orange-red.          p. 5
   **lilacina 'Lilacina'** (Costa Rica), "Blue-flowered teddy-bear"; beautiful pubescent leaves coppery with silver green. Good grower but sensitive to cold.          p. 50
   **reptans** (Guyana); a "Flame violet" with quilted leaves brown-green with silver; blood-red flowers fringed. p. 50
   **reptans 'Lady Lou';** striking foliage bronze with silver, and splashed with rose-pink and white.          p. 9
**ERANTHEMUM** (*Acanthaceae*)
   **nervosum** (India), tropical "Blue sage"; tall stems with dark green leaves and pretty 2 cm blue flowers.          p. 65
**ERICA** (*Ericaceae*)
   **gracilis** (So. Africa), "Rose heath"; shapely little shrub to 30 cm high with tiny needles; loaded autumn to winter with little rosy flowers.          p. 23
   **'Wilmorei',** a "French heather"; pretty 4 cm rosy flowers tipped with white, in winter.          p. 67
**ERVATAMIA** (*Apocynaceae*)
   **coronaria** (India), "Crape jasmine"; glossy green leaves, and waxy white 4–5 cm flowers fragrant at night.     p. 64
**ESPOSTOA** (*Cactaceae*)
   **lanata,** "Peruvian old man"; column beautifully covered with snow-white hair; flowers pinkish.          p. 9, 136
**EUCHARIS** (*Amaryllidaceae*)
   **grandiflora** (Colombia), "Amazon lily"; glossy leaves, and exquisite fragrant white flowers.          p. 28
**EUONYMUS** (*Celastraceae*)
   **fortunei radicans gracilis** (W. China), "Creeping euonymus"; small leathery grayish leaves variegated white. Attractive for terrariums. Winter-hardy.          p. 78
   **japonicus albo-marginatus,** "Silver, leaf euonymus"; smaller, narrower leaves silver-gray, bordered white. p. 9
   **jap. argenteo-variegatus** (Japan), "Silver Queen" in hort.; leathery 4 cm leaves glossy green edged with white. A pretty dishgarden plant.          p. 78
   **jap. aureo-variegatus,** "Yellow Queen" in horticulture; colorful evergreen with leaves richly variegated yellow. Fairly resistant to mildew.          p. 78
   **jap. medio-pictus,** "Goldspot euonymus"; waxy leaves fresh green at margin, golden yellow center and stem. Mildew-prone.          p. 9, 78
   **jap. microphyllus variegatus,** "Variegated box-leaf"; bushy evergreen with tiny 1–2 cm green leaves bordered white. Charming dwarf dishgarden plant.          p. 9, 78

**EUPHORBIA** (*Euphorbiaceae*)

**fulgens** (Mexico), "Scarlet plume"; arching wiry sprays of brilliant 1 cm orange-scarlet bracts, in winter.        p. 67

**ingens** (So. Africa), "Candelabra tree"; tree to 30 ft.; cactus-like, good decorator plant, dark green.        p. 149

**lactea** (India), "Candelabra cactus"; 3–4-angled branches to 5 cm dia., dark green with white marbling.        p. 146, 149

**lactea cristata**, "Elkhorn" or "Frilled fan"; monstrose crested branches forming a snaky ridge; a curiosity plant. A good, durable house plant.        p. 9, 149

**mammillaris** (So. Africa), "Corncob cactus"; tubercled olive green column to 4 cm thick.        p. 147, 149

**mammillaris 'Variegata'**, "Indian corncob"; colorful notched column largely greenish white and tinted pink, with tubercled angles looking like a corn-cob.        p. 149

**polyacantha** (Ethiopia), "Fish bone cactus"; sparry stems 4 cm thick, grayish green with toothed angles.  p. 149

**pulcherrima** (So. Mexico), "Poinsettia"; woody shrub to 4 m tall, with milky juice; foliage deciduous when resting; terminal shoots with showy scarlet bracts, surrounding the tiny yellow flowers; winter-blooming.        p. 67

**pulcherrima 'Ecke Supreme'**, a typical "Poinsettia" or "Christmas star"; large, bright cardinal red bracts during winter time.        p. 15

**splendens** (milii) (W. Madagascar), "Crown of thorns"; spiny shrub with deciduous leaves; flower bracts soft salmon red.        p. 67, 146

**splendens bojeri** (W. Madagascar), "Christ-thorn"; compact habit, gray-spined; persistent dark green 2–4 cm leaves; cardinal red bracts.        p. 149

**tirucalli** (Eastern Africa), "Milk bush" or "Pencil cactus"; slender branches glossy green and bursting with poisonous milk.        p. 149

**trigona**, in hort. as **"hermentiana"** (W. Africa), "African milk tree"; branches to 4 cm thick, rich green prettily marbled white; durable.        p. 149

**EURYA** (*Theaceae*)

**japonica 'Variegata'** (Korea); handsome with glossy, leathery leaves green, beautifully margined white.        p. 9

**x FATSHEDERA** (*Araliaceae*)

**lizei** (Fatsia japonica x Hedera helix), "Ivy tree" or "Botanical wonder"; stem becoming woody, leathery 10–20 cm leaves dark lustrous green.        p. 79

**lizei variegata**, "Variegated pagoda tree"; fresh green leaves prettily edged cream.        p. 123

**FATSIA** (*Araliaceae*)

**japonica** (Japan), "Japanese aralia"; flexible stem with handsome, big glossy green leaves 25–40 cm wide.  p. 73

**FAUCARIA** (*Aizoaceae*)

**tigrina** (So. Africa), "Tiger jaws"; opposite, 3–5 cm long, gray green leaves armed with teeth; flowers yellow.  p. 147

**tuberculosa** (So. Africa), "Pebbled tiger jaws"; wide open jaws of dark green leaves covered with white tubercles. Easy and durable.        p. 150

**FEIJOA** (*Myrtaceae*)

**sellowiana** (Paraguay), "Pineapple guava"; waxy dark green 5–8 cm leaves with white midrib, woolly beneath; white flowers; edible fruit.        p. 62

**FELICIA** (*Compositae*)

**amelloides** (So. Africa), "Blue daisy"; shrubby perennial with 3 cm sky-blue flowers and yellow disk.        p. 62

**FENESTRARIA** (*Aizoaceae*)

**rhopalophylla** (S.W. Africa), "Baby toes"; club-like 2–3 cm leaves bearing translucent window at top; white fl. 4 cm across. Moderate watering only.        p. 150

**FEROCACTUS** (*Cactaceae*)

**latispinus** (Mexico), "Fish-hook barrel"; grayish green globe with curved crimson spines; purplish flowers. p. 139

**FICUS** (*Moraceae*)

**benjamina** (Malaya), "Weeping fig"; gracefully pendant branches, and shining green 8–10 cm leaves; a favorite decorator in tubs.        p. 75

**benjamina 'Exotica'** (Java, Bali), "Java fig"; weeping form with pendulous leaves, slender tips twisted.        p. 75

**carica** (Mediterranean), "Common fig tree"; deeply lobed, rough leaves; sweet, pear-shaped fruit.        p. 71

**diversifolia** (Malaysia), "Mistletoe ficus"; miniature fruiting, with hard dark green 5 cm leaves; bearing small yellowish berries.        p. 76

**dryepondtiana** (Zaïre), "Congo fig"; beautiful quilted 20–30 cm leaves metallic green with purple underside. p. 76

**elastica 'Decora'**, "Wideleaf rubber plant"; broad-leaved seedling of the "India rubber tree"; decorative 25–30 cm leaves deep glossy green; bold decorator plant. Needs good light for best, robust appearance.        p. 9, 77

**elastica 'Doescheri'**, "Variegated rubber plant"; beautiful leathery leaves variegated green, gray, white, pink. Coloring stable not reverting to green.        p. 76

**krishnae** (India, Pakistan), "Sacred fig tree"; leathery leaves in form of cups.        p. 76

**lyrata; pandurata** in hort. (W. Africa), "Fiddleleaf fig"; magnificent decorator with large quilted 30–60 cm leaves deep waxy green.        p. 77

**parcellii** (South Pacific), "Clown fig"; strikingly colorful rough-hairy green leaves, wildly variegated white.        p. 76

**petiolaris** (Mexico), "Blue Mexican fig"; beautiful leathery leaves metallic blue-green, with veins ivory pink to red. Outstanding collector's plant.        p. 76

**pumila (repens** in hort.), "Creeping fig"; small creeper, with tiny 3 cm juv. leaves clinging to walls.        p. 132

**radicans 'Variegata'** (E. Indies), "Variegated rooting fig"; attractive with grayish green leaves variegated white. Requires warmth and moisture.        p. 3, 5, 9, 132

**religiosa** (India), "Sacred Bo-tree" or "Peepul"; gracefully pendant bluish-green leaves with long drip-tip.        p. 76

**retusa** (So. China), the "Chinese banyan"; shapely dense tree with pendant branches; small 8–10 cm leaves. Excellent container floor plant of "weeping" habit.  p. 75

**retusa nitida** (Malaya), "Indian laurel"; resembling laurel with small rubbery, waxy green leaves; good tub plant with light.        p. 75

**rubiginosa variegata** (Queensland), "Miniature rubber plant"; graceful with small 8 cm leaves richly marbled cream. Slow growing; best in a greenhouse.        p. 5, 76

**stricta** (Guam); known in Florida nurseries as "philippinense"; leathery green 15 cm leaves; excellent decorator. Branches broadly arching with pendant foliage.        p. 75

**sycomorus** (N.E. Africa), "Sycamore fig"; rough foliage 8–10 cm long, bluish-green when young.        p. 76

**tikoua** (China), "Waupahu fig"; scandent shrub w. flexible branches, rough 12 cm leaves dark green.        p. 132

**FITTONIA** (*Acanthaceae*)

**verschaffeltii argyroneura** (Peru), "Nerve plant"; charming tropical herb with leaves vivid green netted with white veins.        p. 5, 9, 121

**FORTUNELLA** (*Rutaceae*)

**margarita** (China), "Nagami kumquat" or "Oval kumquat"; shapely bush, willingly bearing oblong golden 4 cm fruit; the white flowers with orange-blossom perfume. p. 70

**FUCHSIA** (*Onagraceae*)

**x hybrida 'Winston Churchill'**, "Lady's eardrops"; excellent pot plant with flowers of salmon sepals and purple double petals.        p. 25

**triphylla 'Gartenmeister Bohnstedt'**, "Honeysuckle fuchsia"; old house plant with bronze foliage and slender flowers salmon rose and scarlet.        p. 31

**GARDENIA**

**jasminoides 'Fortuniana'** (So. China), "Cape jasmine"; large shining leaves and big 10 cm fragrant waxy white double flowers.        p. 64

**jasminoides 'Veitchii'**, "Everblooming gardenia"; charming potplant; dark glossy foliage and double pure white scented flowers.        p. 25

**x GASTERHAWORTHIA** (*Liliaceae*)

**'Royal Higness'**; pretty, small 8–10 cm rosette dark green, densely covered with white warts.        p. 147

**GASTERIA** (*Liliaceae*)

**x Hybrida**, "Oxtongue" or "Bowtie-plant"; thick, tongue-shaped leaves, purplish with pale tubercles.        p. 148

**verrucosa** (So. Africa), "Wart gasteria"; attractive with 2-ranked fleshy leaves covered with white warts.  p. 146

**x GASTROLEA** (*Liliaceae*)

**beguinii** (Aloe in hort.), "Pearl aloe"; pretty rosette of dark green keeled leaves with pale tubercles.        p. 148

**'Spotted Beauty'**, "Gasteria-Aloe hybrid"; attractive, trim miniature to 9 cm dia., deep green with white warts. The hardness of Gasteria with Aloe shape.        p. 9, 147

**GEOGENANTHUS** (*Commelinaceae*)

**undatus** (Peru), "Seersucker plant"; strangely beautiful with fleshy, quilted leaves metallic green banded gray; wine-red beneath.        p. 21, 131

**GERBERA** (*Compositae*)

**jamesonii** (So. Africa), "African daisy" or "Transvaal daisy"; herbaceous perennial with long-lasting flowers in brilliant colors usually orange-scarlet.        p. 62

**GESNERIA** (*Gesneriaceae*)

**cuneifolia** (Cuba), "Fire cracker"; rosette of grass-green leaves, and striking 3 cm tubular fl. burning red. p. 51

**GIBASIS** (*Commelinaceae*)
**geniculata** (**Tradescantia multiflora** in hort.), "Tahitian bridal veil"; good basket plant, dense with small 2 cm leaves olive green, purplish reverse; tiny white fl. Like a bridal veil when covered with blooms.          p. 130

**GIBBAEUM** (*Aizoaceae*)
**petrense** (So. Africa), "Flowering quartz"; minute succulent w. pairs of fat leaves whitish gray green; reddish fl. Must be kept dry when growth is completed.          p. 146

**GLECOMA** (*Labiatae*)
**hederacea variegata** (Temperate Eurasia), better known as Nepeta, the "Variegated ground-ivy"; small, lively creeper with 2–4 cm leaves bordered white.          p. 132

**GLORIOSA** (*Liliaceae*)
**carsonii** (C. Africa); tuberous climber with magnificent flowers wine-purple, edged yellow.          p. 133
**rothschildiana** (Kenya), "Glory-lily"; tendril climber with striking crimson flowers, yellow toward base.          p. 133

**GLOXINIA** (*Gesneriaceae*)
**perennis** (Colombia), "Canterbury-bell gloxinia"; spotted stem bearing spire of downy 3 cm fl. blue with dark throat. Fall-blooming; fragrant of peppermint.          p. 50

**GRAPTOPETALUM** (*Crassulaceae*)
**paraguayense** (Mexico), also known as Sedum weinbergii, "Ghost plant"; amethyst gray w. silvery bloom. p. 147

**GRAPTOPHYLLUM** (*Acanthaceae*)
**pictum** (New Guinea), "Caricature plant"; gay tropical shrub w. leathery purplish leaves splashed w. yellow. p. 122
**pictum albo-marginatum;** variety with leaves variously dark to milky green and gray, variegated white.          p. 122

**GREVILLEA** (*Proteaceae*)
**robusta** (Queensland), "Silk oak"; daintily lacy, green leaves covered w. silky hair; fav. fern-like house plant. p. 79

**GUZMANIA** (*Bromeliaceae*)
**lingulata 'Major'** (Ecuador), "Scarlet star"; spectacular inflorescence of glossy, vivid scarlet bracts from metallic green rosette.          p. 48
**lingulata 'Minor',** "Orange star"; small epiphytic rosette yellow-green; floral bracts orange-red, fl. white. Long-lasting inflorescence.          p. 48
**musaica** (Colombia), "Mosaic vase"; very showy rosette of broad pea-green leaves marked with red-brown cross-bands; orange bracts.          p. 9, 48

**GYMNOCALYCIUM** (*Cactaceae*)
**mihanovichii friedrichii** (Argentina), "Rose-plaid cactus"; little coppery globe to 6 cm., free-flowering pink. p. 9
**mihanovichii friedrichii 'Rubra'** the novel "Red cap", "Oriental moon", "Hibotan"; strikingly colorful small red globe, lacking chlorophyl; usually grafted.          p. 139

**GYNURA** (*Compositae*)
**aurantiaca** (Java), "Velvet plant"; beautiful tropical plant all velvety violet or purple.          p. 114
**bicolor** (Moluccas), "Oakleaved velvet plant" metallic green w. purple sheen, short-hairy on surface; or. fl. p. 131
**'Sarmentosa'** hort. the "Purple passion vine"; creeping stems with soft-fleshy leaves 10 cm long, covered with purple hairs.          p. 131

**HADRODEMAS** (*Commelinaceae*)
**warszewicziana** (Guatemala) (Tripogandra or Spironema in hort.); fleshy pale green rosette resembling dracaena. Clusters of pale purple flowers on long stalk.          p. 131

**HAEMANTHUS** (*Amaryllidaceae*)
**katherinae** (Natal), the "Blood flower"; striking; with fleshy green leaves, solid stalk with head of coral stamens. Beautiful bulbous species for the sunny window.          p. 28

**HAEMARIA** (*Orchidaceae*)
**discolor dawsoniana** (Malaya), "Golden lace orchid"; terrestrial with gorgeous leaves of blackish velvet netted copper; wine-red beneath; small waxy white flowers. p. 53

**HAMATOCACTUS** (*Cactaceae*)
**setispinus** (Mexico, Texas), "Strawberry-cactus"; small 15 cm globe with sunny yellow flowers and red eye. p. 139

**HARRISIA** (*Cactaceae*)
**tortuosa** (Argentina), "Red-tipped dog-tail"; night-bloomer with slender stems; flowers white, 15 cm long. Large edible red fruit.          p. 142

**HAWORTHIA** (*Liliaceae*)
**cuspidata** (So. Africa), "Star window plant"; stocky 6 cm rosette, w. grayish fat leaves, windows at tips. p. 148
**fasciata** (So. Africa), "Zebra haworthia"; pretty 5–8 cm rosette dark green with white tubercles in cross bands. p. 148
**margaritifera** (So. Africa), "Pearl plant"; charming blackish-green rosette, covered with large pearl-like creamy tubercles; tiny whitish flowers.          p. 9, 148
**papillosa** (So. Africa), "Pearly dots"; beautiful with leaves deep green adorned with rows of greenish-white raised often hollow warts.          p. 148

**subfasciata** (Cape Prov.), "Little zebra plant"; shapely rosette dark green, cross-banded with thin rows of white tubercles; popular for dishgardens, very durable.          p. 147

**HEBE** (*Scrophulariaceae*)
**salicifolia** (New Zealand), "Evergreen veronica"; charming evergreen with opposite shining green leaves; purple flowers in spikes.          p. 66

**HEDERA** (*Araliaceae*)
**canariensis 'Variegata',** "Variegated Algerian ivy"; colorful with large 7–14 cm grayish leaves bordered cream and pink; good dishgarden plant.          p. 135
**canar. arborescens 'Variegata',** the "Ghost tree ivy"; woody, arborescent form; durable leaves gray with cream, and black fruit.          p. 5, 9, 78
**canar. 'Gloire de Marengo';** European clone selected for its pronounced variegation; stems and petioles red. Foliage milky green with cream margins.          p. 135
**colchica 'Dentato-variegata'** (Iran), "Variegated Persian ivy"; large variegated leaves to 20 cm, gray-green with apple green.          p. 135
**helix** (Europe, Asia, N. Africa), the popular "English ivy"; glossy forest-green, juv. stage fairly large 7–12 cm lobed leaves; fruiting stage leaves not lobed, the berry-like fruit is black.          p. 135
**helix 'Albany'** "Albany ivy"; self-branching with 9-cm 5-lobed leaves rich green          p.135
**helix 'Hahn's Variegated';** fast growing small-leaved albino with long vines; silver-gray bordered white.          p. 9
**helix 'Harald',** "White and green ivy" or "Improved Chicago variegata"; medium small 4–7 cm leaves green with cream margins.          p. 135
**helix 'Maculata';** slow growing, with large fleshy leaves beautifully variegated dark and nile green with cream. May be form of the Irish ivy.          p. 5
**helix 'Manda's Crested';** good indoor ivy, with star-shaped, jade green leaves, the lobes undulate.          p. 9
**helix 'Manda's Star';** freely vining with large 5-fingered leaves dark green with light veins.          p. 9
**helix 'Patricia';** durable pot plant; dense self-branching with 3–6 cm leaves prettily curled at sinuses.          p. 135
**helix 'Pittsburgh',** the "Pittsburgh ivy"; strong vining with leaves smaller than the English ivy, not as black green; fairly good indoors.          p. 135

**HEDYCHIUM** (*Zingiberaceae*)
**gardnerianum** (Sikkim Himalayas), "Kahili ginger"; beautiful; fragrant yellow flowers with long red filaments. Canes of stiff habit, to 2 m tall.          p. 64

**HELICONIA** (*Musaceae*)
**humilis** (Trinidad), "Lobster claw"; with bold banana-like foliage; spectacular inflorescence of salmon-red bracts and yellowish flowers.          p. 84
**illustris aureo-striata** (South Seas); striking tropical foliage, fresh green with contrasting pink midrib and ivory veins, showing on both surfaces.          p. 84

**HELXINE** (*Urticaceae*)
**soleirolii** (Corsica), "Baby's tears"; low moss-like creeping herb with tiny 6 mm lush green leaves.          p. 132

**HEMIGRAPHIS** (*Acanthaceae*)
**colorata** (Java), tropical "Red ivy"; richly colored prostrate herb with puckered leaves shimmering metallic violet; small white flowers from large bracts.          p. 129
**"Exotica"** hort. (New Guinea), "Purple waffle plant"; robust trailer with 8 cm leaves metallic purplish green on surface, reverse wine-red.          p. 122

**HESPERALOE** (*Liliaceae*)
**parviflora** (Texas to Mexico), "Western aloe" or "Red yucca"; rosette of hard, recurving 1 m leaves; showy salmon-rosy flowers on tall spikes.          p. 85

**HIBISCUS** (*Malvaceae*)
**rosa-sinensis cooperi** (E. Indies), "Checkered hibiscus"; varicolored foliage metallic green, dark olive, white, pink and crimson.          p. 115
**rosa-sinensis 'Matensis',** "Snowflake hibiscus"; willowy red stems dense with rough grayish leaves, variegated creamy-white; fl. red.          p. 115
**rosa-sinensis plenus** (India to China), "Double rose of China"; magnificent flowering bush, large showy 10–15 cm blooms carmine-rose.          p. 65
**rosa-sinensis 'Regius Maximus'** (E. Indies), "Scarlet hibiscus"; vigorous, free-flowering with single 12–18 cm blooms glowing scarlet.          p. 65
**schizopetalus** (E. Africa), "Japanese lantern"; pendulous flowers orange-red with a fantastic long projecting staminal column.          p. 65

**HIPPEASTRUM** (*Amaryllidaceae*)
**leopoldii hyb. 'Claret',** "Dutch amaryllis"; giant glowing crimson trumpet 20 cm dia.; for indoor forcing.          p. 29

**striatum fulgidum** (So. Brazil), "Everblooming amaryllis"; clump-forming, vigorous house plant, recurrent blooms salmon with yellow center. p. 29

**vittatum** (Peru), "Striped amaryllis"; trumpet flower white with purple stripes; needs rest in summer. p. 29

## HOFFMANNIA (*Rubiaceae*)

**ghiesbreghtii** (Mexico), "Taffeta plant"; erect stem with long leaves shimmering velvety bronze, pink ribs. p. 3

**roezlii** (Mexico), "Quilted taffeta plant"; gorgeous quilted foliage, satiny green with rose, wine-red in center; small dark red flowers. Sensitive to chills. p. 121

## HOMALOCLADIUM (*Polygonaceae*)

**platycladum** (Solomon Islands), "Tapeworm plant" or "Ribbon bush"; curiosity plant with flat, fresh-green stems. Small greenish flowers. Good old house plant. p. 78

## HOMALOMENA (*Araceae*)

**wallisii** (Colombia), "Silver shield"; beautiful low, leathery foliage plant dark olive, patterned with silver. A treasure in the exotic collection. p. 5, 96

## HOWEIA (*Palmae*)

**forsteriana** (Lord Howe Is.), "Kentia palm" or "Paradise palm"; elegant, durable decorator tub plant; leathery deep green, graceful fronds. p. 9, 101

## HOYA (*Asclepiadaceae*)

**australis** (E. Australia, Fiji), "Porcelain flower"; robust with broad 8–12 cm leaves glossy green; waxy flowers white with purple. p. 125

**bella** (India), "Miniature wax plant" or "Shower of Stars"; charming plant with 3 cm green leaves, flowers waxy white with purple. p. 125

**carnosa** (Queensland, So. China), the popular "Wax plant"; fragrant waxy pinkish white flowers with red crown; thick-leathery leaves. p. 125

**carnosa 'Tricolor'**, "Krimson Queen" (Plant Pat. 2950) Florida cultivar; charming wax vine with 8 cm leaves green w. ivory; young fol. copper, edged with rose and red. p. 2

**carnosa variegata**, "Variegated wax plant"; fresh green leathery leaves bordered cream-white, often edged red. Tolerates neglect. Ideal for dishgardens. p. 9, 125

**engleriana** (Thailand), in horticulture as H. minima or Dischidia; small round $1\frac{1}{2}$ cm grayish leaves; flowers pink with crimson. p. 125

**imperialis** (Borneo), "Honey plant"; robust climber with waxy flowers reddish brown, crown creamy-white. Shiny leaves to 20 cm long; wavy. p. 125

**kerrii** (Thailand), "Sweetheart hoya"; thick inverted heart-shaped leaves; small velvety flowers greenish, tinted pink; crown crimson. p. 125

**motoskei** (Sumatra), "Spotted hoya"; robust climber with leaves spotted silver; star-like flowers pinkish with maroon. Very tolerant house plant. p. 125

**purpureo-fusca** (Java), "Silver-pink vine"; leaves waxy green with raised pinkish silver blotching; rusty red flowers with pink and purple. p. 125

## HUERNIA (*Asclepiadaceae*)

**zebrina** (Botswana), "Owl eyes"; reddish stems with stout teeth; starlike 4 cm yellow fl. with purple bands. p. 151

## HYACINTHUS (*Liliaceae*)

**'Pink Pearl'** (orientalis cv.); excellent early bl. hyacinth, lovely vivid pink; old favorite for Easter. p. 27

## HYDRANGEA (*Saxifragaceae*)

**macrophylla 'Merveille'**, a French "Hortensia", or "Snowballs"; robust variety with large heads to 20 cm dia. of carmine-rose flowers of good texture. p. 15

**macrophylla 'Strafford'**, originated in France as 'Mad. Cayeux'; exceptional, with dark foliage and firm heads clear rosy-red. p. 24

## HYDROSME (*Araceae*)

**rivieri** (Vietnam), in hort. as Amorphophallus, the sinister "Devil's tongue"; from large tuber rises a 1 m floral spike with reddish spadix and puple spathe, with offensive odor; foliage after flowering. p. 98

## HYLOCEREUS (*Cactaceae*)

**undatus** (Brazil), "Honolulu queen"; one of largest night-bloomers, with white flowers to 30 cm long. p. 142

## HYMENOCALLIS (*Amaryllidaceae*)

**narcissiflora** (Ismene calathina) (Bolivia), "Basket flower"; two-edged floral stalk with large white, very fragrant flowers. p. 28

## HYPOESTES (*Acanthaceae*)

**sanguinolenta** (Madagascar), "Freckle-face"; delicate tropical herb with soft green leaves splashed and spotted rosy-red; small lilac flowers. p. 121

## ILEX (*Aquifoliaceae*)

**cornuta 'Burfordii'**, "Chinese holly"; bushy form with shining 5 cm vivid green leaves and few spines; scarlet berries on female plants. p. 79

## IMPATIENS (*Balsaminaceae*)

**hawkeri 'Exotica'** (New Guinea); beautiful foliage plant w. red stalk and gayly colored foliage green, yellow and crimson; flower rose. p. 30

**oliveri** (E. Africa), "Giant touch-me-not"; succulent leaves olive green and pale midrib; spurred 4–6 cm flower lilac pink. p. 30

**platypetala aurantiaca** (Celebes), "Tangerine impatiens"; charming with fresh green leaves w. pink midrib; orange-yellow flowers with red eye. p. 30

**walleriana var. holstii** (E. Africa), "Busy Lizzie"; water-succulent herb with small coppery leaves; fiery scarlet 3–4 cm flowers. p. 30

**walleriana var. sultanii 'Variegata'** (Zanzibar), "Variegated patient Lucy"; old-fashioned window plant with milky leaves bordered white; carmine-red flowers bloom continuously. p. 30

## IOCHROMA (*Solanaceae*)

**tubulosum** (Colombia), "Violet bush"; hairy shrub with downy leaves, pendulous purple 4 cm flowers tipped lavender. Ideal for summer patio or roof garden. p. 65

## IPOMOEA (*Convolvulaceae*)

**batatas 'Blackie'** (E. Indies), "Blackleaf sweet-potato"; window vine with brown stem, and leaves black-purple, wine-red beneath; from tuberous edible roots. p. 131

## IRESINE (*Amaranthaceae*)

**herbstii 'Aureo-reticulata'** (Brazil), "Chicken-gizzard"; colorful window plant with notched leaves fresh green with yellow veins. p. 30

**lindenii formosa** (Ecuador), "Yellow bloodleaf"; attractive window plant with narrow 5–8 cm leaves yellow and green, red petioles and stem. p. 5

## IXIA (*Iridaceae*)

**x 'Rose Queen'** (So. Africa), "Corn-lily"; small cormous plant with grasslike leaves, and starry 4–5 cm flowers soft pink opening with the warming sun. p. 27

## IXORA (*Rubiaceae*)

**javanica** (Java), "Jungle geranium"; small flowering shrub with leathery foliage, and clusters of waxy salmon-red blossoms. Good pot plant though blooms soon drop. p. 68

## JACOBINIA (*Acanthaceae*)

**velutina** (Brazil), "Brazilian plume"; striking fountain-like trusses of arched rosy blooms, above soft-hairy olive green leaves. p. 63

## JASMINUM (*Oleaceae*)

**grandiflorum** (Kashmir), "Spanish jasmine" or "Poet's jasmine"; straggling bush with showy white, fragrant 4 cm flowers, reddish beneath. p. 126

**mesnyi (primulinum)** (China), "Primrose jasmine"; rambling shrub, shining green leaves, and showy yellow flowers to 5 cm dia. p. 126

**nitidum** (So. Pacific), "Angelwing jasmine"; semi-vining with shining green leaves; large 4 cm glistening white, fragrant flowers. p. 126

**polyanthum** (China), "Pink jasmine"; freely blooming with masses of deliciously scented 2 cm flowers white within, rose outside. p. 126

**rex** (Thailand), "King jasmine"; exquisite with large, pure white 5 cm flowers; hard foliage dark green. p. 126

**sambac** (Arabia, India), "Arabian jasmine"; woody clamberer with firm green leaves; powerfully fragrant, gardenia like white flowers. ($2\frac{1}{2}$ cm). p. 64

**sambac 'Grand Duke'**, "Gardenia jasmine"; a ball-shaped form with tightly double waxy-white blooms to 4 cm dia., with intense sweet fragrance. p. 64

**simplicifolium** (South Seas), "Little star jasmine"; rambling shrub with glossy leaves; sweetly fragrant tiny $1\frac{1}{2}$ cm star-flowers white. p. 126

## JUSTICIA (*Acanthaceae*)

**extensa** (Africa: Zaïre), attractive shrubby plant with papery fresh green leaves splashed with silver. p. 122

## KAEMPFERIA (*Zingiberaceae*)

**pulchra** (Burma), "Resurrection lily"; ornate broad bronze leaves with gray bands; fleeting blue flower from fleshy rhizome. p. 84

**roscoeana** (Burma), "Peacock plant"; foliage beautiful as shining bronzy taffeta, iridescently zoned pale green like a peacock; purple flower. p. 122

## KALANCHOE (*Crassulaceae*)

**blossfeldiana 'Tom Thumb'**, "Flaming Katy"; cheerful plant with masses of brilliant scarlet flowers in winter; succulent bronzy green foliage. p. 23

**'Daigremontiana hybrid'** (daigr. x tubiflora), the "Good-luck plant"; prolific with fleshy, narrow pinkish-brown leaves about 5 cm long, spotted purple; young plantlets form on margins. p. 9

**fedtschenkoi** (Madagascar), "Purple scallops"; small 3 cm leaves notched at apex, delicately glaucous amethyst edged with purple; rosy flower. p. 146

**fedtschenkoi 'Marginata'** (California), "Aurora Borealis plant"; charming sport pale bluish gray attractively margined creamy white. p. 147

**gastonis-bonnieri** (Madagascar), a "Life plant" with large coppery leaves 12–18 cm long, covered with white-mealy powder; flowers pink. Young plants develop at leaf tips. A good houseplant; conversation piece. p. 150

**marmorata** (Ethiopia), "Pen wiper plant"; flaccid 6–10 cm leaves pinkish to glaucous blue and blotched with purple; flower white. p. 9, 146

**pinnata**, in horticulture as **Bryophyllum** (Trop. Africa), the "Airplant" or "Miracle leaf"; fleshy leaves tinged with red. Produces plantlets at edges, even when separated leaf is hung on a curtain. p. 150

**'Roseleaf'** (beharensis x tomentosa); attractive triangular leaves about 5 to 8 cm long, with brown felt above and silver beneath; teeth brown. p.146

**tomentosa** (C. Madagascar), the beautiful "Panda plant"; soft fleshy 8 cm leaves entirely clothed in dense white felt, with brown marginal teeth. p. 5, 9, 145, 146

**KOHLERIA** (Gesneriaceae)

**'Eriantha hybrid'**, known in hort. as **Isoloma hirsutum**; green leaves bordered by red hairs; inflated flowers orange-red 2 cm long; willing bloomer. p. 50

**lindeniana** (Ecuador), a beautiful "Tree gloxinia"; velvety leaves vivid green with silvery veins; white bell-flowers with purple throat. p. 50

**tubiflora** (Costa Rica), "Painted kohleria"; hairy plant with green leaves red beneath; 2½ cm flowers orange marked with red. p. 50

**LACHENALIA** (Liliaceae)

**lilacina** (So. Africa), "Cape cowslip"; small bulbous plant with foliage spotted purple; lavender flowers in oblong spike. p. 29

**LAELIA** (Orchidaceae)

**perrinii** (Brazil), an elegant "Amalia", with clusters of 12 cm flowers light rose, the lip intensely purplish crimson. Cattleya-like blooms in autumn-winter. p. 58

**purpurata** (Brazil), known as "Queen of orchids"; magnificent epiphyte with showy clusters of 15 cm flowers glistening white, lip crimson, throat yellow. p. 58

**LAMIUM** (Labiatae)

**galeobdolon variegatum** (Quebec to Urals), the "Silver nettle vine"; rampant threadlike stems with rough leaves to 5 cm, prettily zoned silver over green. p. 132

**LANTANA** (Verbenaceae)

**camara** (W. Indies), "Shrub verbena"; popular window plant with bristly leaves and heads of flowers in colors pink, yellow, orange. p. 25

**LEMAIREOCEREUS** (Cactaceae)

**beneckei**, "Chalk candle"; slender column coated with white waxy powder; flowers white and brown. p. 136

**LEUCHTENBERGIA** (Cactaceae)

**principis** (Mexico), "Prism-cactus" or "Agave cactus"; to 20 cm high; unusual with grayish elongate tubercles looking like agave leaves; yellow flower. p. 139

**LIGULARIA** (Compositae)

**tussilaginea argentea**, "Silver farfugium"; basal rosette with attractive soft-leathery leaves, grayish and variegated white. p. 114

**tussilaginea aureo-maculata** (Japan), also known as **Farfugium**, the "Leopard plant"; large rounded green leaves blotched yellow; daisy-like yellow flower. p. 114

**LIGUSTRUM** (Oleaceae)

**lucidum 'Texanum'** (orig. Japan), "Waxleaf privet"; with shiny leathery leaves 6–8 cm long; ideal for shaping as decorator plant. p. 73

**LILIUM** (Liliaceae)

**longiflorum 'Croft'** (Oregon 1928), an American "Easter lily"; elegant, firm-textured white trumpets 15 cm long; ideal for Easter forcing in pots. p. 15

**LIRIOPE** (Liliaceae)

**muscari 'Variegata'** (Japan), "Lily-turf"; tufting grass-like; leathery rich green leaves with yellow margins; flowers lilac. p. 86

**LITHOPS** (Aizoaceae)

**bella** (S.W. Africa), "Stone face"; small 3 cm succulent body with fissure across top, beige with darker markings; white flowers. p. 151

**karasmontana** (S.W. Africa), "Mountain pebble"; club-shaped cleft body pearl-gray, top brownish; fl. white. p. 151

**marmorata** (Cape Prov.), "Marble plant"; buff body with marble design of translucent brown on cleft surface; flower white. p. 146

**pseudotruncatella** (S.W. Africa), a "Living stone"; split rocks with surface brownish-gray and network of brown lines; 3 cm flower yellow. p. 151

**LIVISTONA** (Palmae)

**chinensis, "Latania borbonica"** of hort. (So. China), "Chinese fan palm"; wide-spreading crown of glossy, fresh green, plaited fronds, the tips hanging. p. 102

**LOBIVIA** (Cactaceae)

**aurea** (No. Argentina), "Golden lily-cactus" or "Cob cactus"; lovely small window sill plant to 10 cm high, with yellowish spines; profuse blooms glossy yellow. p. 136

**LOPEZIA** (Onagraceae)

**lineata** (Mexico)," Mosquito flower"; charming small window plant with curious insect-like 1 cm winged red flowers bearing hard gland resembling "drop of honey". p. 64

**LOPHOPHORA** (Cactaceae)

**williamsii** (So. Texas, Mexico), "Sacred mushroom" or "Peyote"; small globe to 8 cm dia., bluish green; flowers pink to white. p. 142

**LYCASTE** (Orchidaceae)

**aromatica** (Guatemala), attractive dwarf epiphyte with fragrant, waxy 8 cm blooms greenish with gold lip. p. 58

**deppei** (So. Mexico); good house plant, with waxy long-lasting flowers greenish-yellow spotted red; petals white. In bloom nearly all year. p. 58

**virginalis alba** (Guatemala), "White Nun orchid"; handsome, profusely blooming with large waxy 15 cm flowers pure white and very fragrant. p. 58

**LYCOPERSICON** (Solanaceae)

**esculentum 'Tiny Tim'**, a miniature "Cherry tomato"; cute little plant freely bearing small round 2 cm scarlet fruit in the sunny kitchen window. p. 70

**LYGODIUM** (Filices)

**japonicum** (Japan to Himalayas), a "Climbing fern"; twining thread-like stems bearing dainty fronds of pretty green; the fertile pinnae more lacy. p. 110

**MALPIGHIA** (Malpighiaceae)

**coccigera** (W. Indies), a pretty "Miniature holly"; tiny 2 cm leaves glossy dark green with spiny teeth; lovely starry pink flowers. p. 78

**MALVAVISCUS** (Malvaceae)

**penduliflorus** (Mexico), "Turk's cap" or "Sleepy mallow"; large hibiscus-like leaves, and showy, pendulous 5 cm flowers, brilliant red. p. 65

**MAMMILLARIA** (Cactaceae)

**bocasana** (Mexico), "Powder puff"; looking like a bursting cotton ball, 5 cm dia., covered with snow-white hair; flowers creamy-white. p. 138

**compressa** (C. Mexico), "Mother of hundreds"; small bluish-green globe, forming clumps; flowers pinkish. p. 138

**elongata** (Mexico), "Golden stars"; small clustering cylinders to 3 cm thick, light green with yellow spines; flower white. p. 138

**fragilis** (Mexico), "Thimble-cactus"; freely branching, to 10 cm high, bright green covered with white radial spines. Flowers cream, purplish outside. p. 138

**geminispina** (C. Mexico), known "Whitey"; handsome small club-shaped cactus, bluish-glaucous with white spines; flower red. p. 9, 138

**magnimamma** (C. Mexico), "Mexican pincushion"; dark green 10 cm globe with conic tubercles topped by white wool; creamy flower. p. 138

**MANETTIA** (Rubiaceae)

**inflata**, in hort. as **bicolor** (Uruguay), "Firecracker plant"; twining herb with green leaves and 2 cm tubular waxy flowers vivid yellow with scarlet bristles. p. 129

**MANIHOT** (Euphorbiaceae)

**esculenta variegata** (Brazil), "Cassava" or "Tapioca plant"; known for its starchy tubers; foliage fresh green variegated yellow. p. 123

**MARANTA** (Marantaceae)

**arundinacea variegata** (Mexico), "Variegated arrow-root"; slender erect herb with starchy roots; zigzag branches with green and white foliage. p. 116

**leuconeura erythroneura** (Brazil), "Red-veined prayer plant"; beautiful leaves velvety olive, jagged silver center and red veins. p. 116

**leuconeura kerchoveana** (Brazil), well-known "Prayer plant"; foliage pale green with two rows of chocolate blotches; leaves fold upward in the evening. p. 9, 116

**leuconeura massangeana** (Brazil), "Rabbit's foot"; strikingly beautiful having satiny bluish-green leaves with silver and pink and zones of brown. p. 5, 9, 116

**MARSILEA** (Filices)

**drummondii** (W. Australia), "Hairy water clover"; aquatic perennial with floating 4-parted clover-like leaves 8 cm dia., covered with white hairs. p. 112

**MASDEVALLIA** (*Orchidaceae*)
**veitchiana** (Andes of Peru at 4000 m), a "Tailed orchid"; weird, striking epiphyte with brilliant orange-scarlet 15 cm flowers, the upper sepal with long tail.                    p. 59
**MAXILLARIA** (*Orchidaceae*)
**picta** (Brazil); bushy epiphyte free-blooming with fragrant 6 cm flowers yellow, purple, chocolate; white lip.                                                                           p. 59
**MEDINILLA** (*Melastomaceae*)
**magnifica** (Philippines), "Rose grape"; spectacular flowering shrub with decorative leaves, and striking pendant inflorescence of showy pink bracts and red flower.      p. 63
**MENTHA** (*Labiatae*)
**requienii** (Corsica), "Corsican mint"; miniature spreading herb with tiny bright green leaves strongly peppermint-scented. Leaves used for flavoring.                    p. 132
**MICONIA** (*Melastomaceae*)
**magnifica** (calvescens) (Mexico), "Velvet tree"; tropical foliage plant with beautiful leaves to 75 cm long, velvety green with ivory ribs, purple beneath.              p. 123
**MIKANIA** (*Compositae*)
**ternata** (Brazil), "Plush vine"; attractive, rapid trailer with 4 cm leaves coppery green, purple beneath, densely covered with white hair.                              p. 133
**MILTONIA** (*Orchidaceae*)
**roezlii alba** (Panama), a lovely "Pansy orchid"; exquisite open face, 8–10 cm flowers pure white.        p. 59
**MIMOSA** (*Leguminosae*)
**pudica** (Brazil), "Sensitive plant" or "Touch-me-not"; feathery grass-green leaves which fold their segments when touched; flowers like purple puffs.                  p. 120
**MIMULUS** (*Scrophulariaceae*)
**aurantiacus**, syn. Diplacus glutinosus (Oregon, California), the "Monkey-flower"; shrubby with sticky branches and 2-lipped flowers orange-salmon.                     p. 68
**MONSTERA** (*Araceae*)
**deliciosa** (So. Mexico), "Mexican breadfruit"; its juvenile stage known as Philodendron pertusum as grown in tubs. Stout climber with distinctive glossy green leaves cut and perforated with oblong holes; cone-like edible fruit. Popular decorator.                          p. 14, 72, 87
**obliqua expilata,** (Alto Amazonas), a "Window-leaf"; a sculptor's dream—interesting green foliage perforated with holes down to a bare skeleton.               p. 87
**pertusa** (Guyana), known as "Marcgravia paradoxa"; lush climber with soft, perforated leaves.           p. 87
**MURRAYA** (*Rutaceae*)
**exotica** (India to Philippines), "Orange jessamine"; handsome with glossy green leaves and small white, fragrant flowers, succeeded by 1 cm vivid red berries. p. 72
**MUSA** (*Musaceae*)
**nana** (cavendishii) (So. China), "Chinese dwarf banana"; of compact habit suitable for tubs; glaucous green foliage; produces aromatic edible, yellow fruit.      p. 71, 84
**x paradisiaca** (India), "Common banana"; tree-like herb to 8 m tall, with slender trunk and great, fraying leaves; yellow fruit.                                            p. 84
**zebrina** (Java), "Blood banana"; slender plant with tall trunk bearing leaves satiny bluish green richly painted with blood red; underside red.                            p. 84
**MUSCARI** (*Liliaceae*)
**armeniacum 'Heavenly Blue'** (Turkey), the "Grape hyacinth"; charming bulbous plant with spires of nodding flowers azure-blue.                                  p. 27
**MYRSINE** (*Myrsinaceae*)
**africana** (No. Africa to Himalaya), "African boxwood"; resembling Buxus but more graceful; red stems, small shiny dark leaves; blue berries on female plants.       p. 78
**MYRTILLOCACTUS** (*Cactaceae*)
**geometrizans** (S. Mexico), "Blue myrtle cactus"; handsome slender columns glaucous blue, with branches sparry; small greenish flowers.                      p. 137
**MYRTUS** (*Myrtaceae*)
**communis microphylla** (E. Mediterranean), "German myrtle"; densely leafy shrub with tiny shining black green 2 cm overlapping leaves and white aromatic flowers; can be sheared into globes.                            p. 78
**NARCISSUS** (*Amaryllidaceae*)
**pseudo-narcissus 'King Alfred';** a large-flowered "Trumpet daffodil"; large golden-yellow flowers 10 cm across; for Easter blooming. Hardy.              p. 27
**NEOMARICA** (*Iridaceae*)
**northiana** (Brazil), "Walking iris", "Apostle plant" or "Marica" in hort. Leaves in flat fan; fragrant fl. 7–10 cm across, with white outer petals marked brown, inner segments tipped violet. Young plantlets develop from floral spike.                                          p. 28

**NEOREGELIA** (*Bromeliaceae*)
**carolinae 'Marechalii'** (Brazil), "Blushing bromeliad"; flattened rosette of metallic green leaves; at flowering time inner leaves turn brilliant crimson; fl. purple.      p. 46
**carolinae 'Tricolor'**, "Striped blushing bromeliad"; attractive mutant with glossy green leaves having ivory bands lengthwise.                               p. 46
**farinosa** (Brazil), called "Crimson cup" because at flowering time the short inner leaves turn vivid crimson; outer leaves olive.                                  p. 46
**x 'Mar-Con'** (marmorata x concentrica), "Marbled fingernail"; bold rosette of apple-green leaves overlaid with pattern of red-purple, tips red.                     p. 46
**x 'Marmorata hybrid'**, "Marbled fingernail plant"; light olive green, stiff leaves blotched maroon and with red tips; lavender flower deep in center cup.            p. 46
**mooreana** (Amazonian Peru), "Ossifragi vase"; tubular rosette of glossy grass green leaves recoiling at tips; margins with black spines.                              p. 46
**sarmentosa chlorosticta** (Brazil); small rosette of bright green leaves overlaid by maroon marbling; lavender flower.                                            p. 46
**spectabilis** (Brazil), "Fingernail plant"; an old favourite with olive green leaves, gray crossbands, and red tips; blue flowers in low center cushion.                  p. 46
**tristis** (Brazil), "Miniature marble plant"; dwarf rosette deep olive green and mottled maroon, tips red.      p. 46
**NEPENTHES** (*Nepenthaceae*)
**x atrosanguinea**, a tropical "Pitcher plant" of Malaysian origin; carnivorous plant with slender pitchers rich maroon over greenish yellow.                             p. 3
**NEPHROLEPIS** (*Filices*)
**biserrata** (ensifolia hort.) (Cuba to Peru, Polynesia etc.), "Bold sword fern"; large arching fresh green, leathery fronds 1 m long; leaflets sickle-shaped.        p. 107
**cordifolia 'Plumosa'** (Japan to New Zealand), "Dwarf whitmanii" in hort.; bushy, attractive feather-fern with stiff, dark green fronds, bearing viable spores.          p. 107
**exaltata** (wide-spread in world tropics), the ubiquitous "Swordfern"; tufted fern with stiffly erect green fronds simply divided.                                      p. 107
**exaltata bostoniensis compacta**, "Dwarf Boston fern"; an old time house plant, compact but with fresh green fronds larger and wider than the species, all sterile; segments wavy.                                    p. 107
**exaltata 'Fluffy Ruffles'**, "Dwarf feather fern"; small and dense feathery fronds under 30 cm, close together, dark green.                                          p. 107
**exaltata 'Hillii'**, "Crisped featherfern"; excellent strong growing variety with broad segments overlapping and wavy, or deeply lobed and crisped.                 p. 107
**exaltata 'Rooseveltii plumosa'**, "Tall feather-fern"; largest form of the feathered type, rather leathery, fronds to 1 m long.                                           p. 107
**exaltata 'Verona'**, "Verona lace fern"; dwarf tripinnate variety with delicate, very lacy fronds.        p. 107
**exaltata 'Whitmanii';** popular "Feather fern" of open habit, the broad light green fronds feathery with small segments.                                           p. 107
**NEPHTHYTIS** (*Araceae*)
**gravenreuthii** (Cameroon); broadly halberd-shaped yellow green leaves with dark veining.               p. 98
**NERIUM**
**oleander 'Carneum florepleno'**, "Mrs. Roeding oleander"; evergreen shrub with willowy branches and dark green, leathery leaves; topped by clusters of double flowers salmon pink; well-known decorator tub plant. p. 79
**NERTERA** (*Rubiaceae*)
**granadensis** (depressa) (Peru to New Zealand), "Coral-bead plant" or "Hardy baby tears"; enchanting mat-forming creeper with tiny green leaves; berries orange-red.                                         p. 72
**NICODEMIA** (*Loganiaceae*)
**diversifolia** (Madagascar), "Indoor oak"; bushy plant with quilted, lobed foliage iridescent metallic-blue.  p. 123
**NIDULARIUM** (*Bromeliaceae*)
**innocentii nana** (Brazil), "Miniature birdsnest", small rosette of olive green leaves glossy purple underside, the inner nest turns orange red; flower white.        p. 48
**NOPALXOCHIA** (*Cactaceae*)
**ackermannii 'Fire Glory'** (Mexico); beautiful "Orchid cactus" with large 10 cm flowers soft rosy-scarlet. p. 141
**phyllanthoides** (Mexico: Puebla), "German Empress"; free-flowering epiphyte with a profusion of medium-size carmine-rose flowers; lovely basket plant.        p. 141

**NOTOCACTUS** (*Cactaceae*)

**haselbergii** (So. Brazil), a "Ball cactus"; lovely small globe to 8 cm, covered with silvery-white spines; flowers orange-red.                              p. 139

**rutilans** (Argentina), "Pink ball cactus"; tiny dark green globe, dwarfed by big 6 cm silky flowers bright pink with yellow throat.                              p. 139

**NYCTOCEREUS** (*Cactaceae*)

**serpentinus** (Mexico), "Snake-cactus", a "Queen of the night"; slender cylindric night-bloomer with pale spines, and large white, sweet-scented flowers.            p. 142

**OCHNA** (*Ochnaceae*)

**serrulata** (So. Africa), "Mickey-mouse plant"; woody shrub with hard-leathery foliage and flowers with yellow petals followed by black berry-like fruits.          p. 62

**ODONTOGLOSSUM** (*Orchidaceae*)

**crispum** (Colombia), the "Lace orchid"; exquisitely beautiful, with arching sprays of waxy, crisped 6–9 cm flowers glistening white, lip marked red.          p. 60

**grande** (Mexico), "Tiger orchid"; beautiful with waxy 10–15 cm flowers yellow barred with brown.          p. 60

**pulchellum** (Mexico), "Lily of the valley orchid"; charming with small waxy, sweetly fragrant 2–3 cm flowers white.                              p. 60

**OLEA** (*Oleaceae*)

**europaea** (E. Mediterranean), the classical "Olive tree"; woody evergreen wtih leathery gray green leaves, fragrant flowers, and bearing plum-like tart fruit.          p. 71

**ONCIDIUM** (*Orchidaceae*)

**flexuosum** (Brazil), a "Dancing doll orchid"; profuse with arching sprays of gay 3 cm flowers bright golden yellow barred with brown.                  p. 59

**lanceanum** (Venezuela), "Leopard orchid"; beautiful with vanilla-scented 5 cm fleshy flowers yellow, green, violet, rose and chocolate.                  p. 59

**sarcodes** (Brazil); vigorous epiphyte handsome with large 5 cm glossy flowers yellow with brown.          p. 59

**sphacelatum** (C. America), the "Golden shower orchid"; prolific epiphyte with giant sprays of many pretty 3 cm yellow and brown flowers looking like dolls.          p. 59

**splendidum** (C. America); robust epiphyte with large substantial and long lasting 8 cm flowers yellow, barred with brown on petals and sepals.                  p. 59

**stipitatum** (C. America); drooping inflorescence dense with small 3 cm sulphur-yellow flowers marked red.  p. 59

**OPHIOPOGON** (*Liliaceae*)

**jaburan** (Japan), "White lily-turf"; clump-forming with grass-like, leathery dark green leaves; white flowers. p. 86

**jaburan 'Variegatus'**, "Variegated Mondo"; attractive form which I collected in Java; with linear leaves milky-green, striped and edged in white.                  p. 86

**japonicus** (Japan, Korea), "Snake's beard"; grass-like with very narrow, leathery, blackish-green leaves 15–25 cm long; small lilac flowers.                  p. 86

**OPLISMENUS** (Gramineae)

**hirtellus variegatus** (W. Indies), in hort. as "Panicum", the "Basket grass", creeping, pretty tropical grass daintily striped white and pink.                  p. 86

**OPUNTIA** (*Cactaceae*)

**basilaris** (Utah to New Mexico), "Beaver tail"; fleshy bluish-coppery pads to 20 cm, almost spineless; showy, variable flowers usually purplish.                  p. 138

**brasiliensis** (Brazil, Bolivia), "Tropical tree-opuntia"; branching tree-like; friendly green, elongate glossy joints almost spineless; yellow flowers.                  p. 140

**cylindrica** (Ecuador, Peru), "Emerald idol"; succulent cylindrical, dark green joints 5 cm thick with little leaves deciduous when resting; flowers scarlet.          p. 138

**erinacea ursina** (California), the famous "Grizzly bear" of the Mohave; grayish, flattened 10–15 cm joints densely covered with long white spines; fl. red or yellow.  p. 140

**ficus-indica** (prob. Mexico), the "Indian fig"; large oblong 20–60 cm joints green or glaucous with irritating yellow bristles; fl. yellow; edible orange fruit.      p. 72

**ficus-indica 'Burbank'**, the "Spineless Indian fig"; bold, elongate, smooth joints bluish green to ½ m long, practically spineless.                  p. 9, 140

**fulgida mamillata monstrosa** (Arizona, Mexico), "Boxing-glove"; cylindrical knobby joints somewhat contorted; sharp yellow spines; flower pink.          p. 140

**leucotricha** (C. Mexico), "White-hair tree-cactus"; branching with flat, oblong joints to 25 cm long, covered with long flexible white spines; flower yellow.          p. 138

**linguiformis 'Maverick'**, "Maverick cactus"; California mutant; flat green joint develops a multitude of monstrose branchlets, resembling a miniature tree.          p. 140

**microdasys** (No. Mexico), called "Bunny ears" because young pads look ear-like; satiny green pads covered with tufts of yellow bristles.                  p. 9, 138

**microdasys albispina**, "Polka-dots"; pads with pure white tufted hairs (glochids), flowers yellow.          p. 138

**rufida** (Texas, No. Mexico), "Cinnamon-cactus"; fleshy pads velvety grayish green covered with tufts of short brown bristles which rub off.                  p. 138

**schickendantzii** (No. Argentina), "Lion's tongue"; attractive elongate, flattened joints green with sparse reddish spines; flower yellow. Popular in dishgardens.      p. 140

**subulata** (Chile), "Eve's-pin cactus"; smooth, bright green cylindric stems with persistent awl-shaped leaves but few spines; flower orange.                  p. 138

**tomentosa** (Mexico), "Velvet opuntia"; thick-fleshy long joints velvet green; flower yellow, followed by red fruit along apex.                  p. 140

**vilis** (Mexico), "Little tree-cactus"; little plant with short cylindric joints branching at top, covered by whitish spines; red flowers.                  p. 138

**vulgaris**, known in hort. as **monacantha** (So. Brazil), "Irish mittens"; attractive flattened, glossy green joints nearly spineless; fl. yellow. Unripened fruit will root if planted, and sprout "ears".                  p. 140

**vulgaris variegata**, known as "Joseph's coat"; a pretty, variegated form with smooth joints beautifully marbled white or pink.                  p. 140

**OREOCEREUS** (*Cactaceae*)

**celsianus** (Bolivia), the attractive "Old man of the Andes" cylindrical cactus with long white hairs and thin red spines; flower red.                  p. 136

**ORNITHOGALUM** (*Liliaceae*)

**caudatum** (So. Africa), "False sea-onion" or "Healing onion"; old-fashioned house plant with big green bulb; small white 3 cm flowers striped green. Used for bruises or colds in home medicine.                  p. 29

**OSMANTHUS** (*Oleaceae*)

**fragrans** (Himalayas to Japan), "Sweet olive" or "Fragrant olive"; handsome evergreen with glossy olive-green 5–10 cm leaves finely toothed; clusters of small white flowers strongly fragrant of jasmine.          p. 79

**heterophyllus 'Variegatus'** (Japan), "Variegated false holly"; dense evergreen very attractive with small holly-like spiny leaves grayish green edged in white.      p. 5, 79

**OXALIS** (*Oxalidaceae*)

**bowiei** (So. Africa), "Giant pink clover"; bulbo-tuberous; fleshy leaves with 3 waxy light green segments; big 3–5 cm beautiful rosy-carmine flower.                  p. 124

**braziliensis** (Brazil), one of "Shamrocks" of florists; bulbous with shimmering green 3-parted leaves; large 3 cm flower magenta and crimson.                  p. 124

**deppei** (So. Mexico), "Lucky clover" or "Good luck plant"; bulbous plant bearing leaves with 4 leaflets zoned purplish; flower rosy red.                  p. 124

**hedysaroides rubra** (Ecuador); the gorgeous "Fire-fern"; wiry stems with fern-like foliage of glowing, satiny wine-red; little bright yellow flowers.          p. 124

**martiana 'Aureo-reticulata'** (Trop. America), "Gold-net sour clover"; attractive ornamental with scaly bulb; large 8 cm leaves fresh green, reticulated with yellow; flower rose with red lines from white throat.          p. 124

**ortgiesii** (Peru), "Tree oxalis"; handsome with succulent stem and maroon-red fishtail leaves; small yellow flowers. Curiosity plant with its unusual foliage.  p. 124

**pes-caprae** (So. Africa), "Bermuda buttercup"; handsome flowering plant from scaly bulb; nodding yellow flowers to 4 cm dia.                  p. 124

**purpurea** (So. Africa), in hort. as "Grand duchess oxalis"; blackish bulb; fresh green foliage to 8 cm dia., showy, pretty 5 cm flowers bright rose with yellow. p. 124

**PACHYPHYTUM** (*Crassulaceae*)

**'Blue Haze'**; attractive with thick-fleshy, smooth leaves glaucous blue with red tips; flower yellow.          p. 9

**compactum** (Mexico), "Thick plant"; lovely little "hard" succulent with thick leaves suffused with brown, and silvery-white glaucous.                  p. 147

**'Cornelius'**, "Moonstones"; a "hard" succulent, glaucous olive green with red apex; flowers tipped red.  p. 147

**PACHYSTACHYS** (*Acanthaceae*)

**coccinea** (Brazil), also known as Jacobinia, "Cardinal's guard"; shrubby plant with rough 20 cm leaves; dense terminal head of scarlet flowers.                  p. 68

**lutea** (Peru), "Gold-hops", introduced in Europe as Beloperone "Super Goldy"; striking inflorescence of shingled orange bracts, bursting with white flowers.      p. 68

**x PACHYVERIA** (*Crassulaceae*)
　**'Curtis',** known as "White cloud"; very pretty, "hard" bluish-green rosette covered with silvery bloom, the tips red. A very pretty succulent.　　　　p. 148

**PALISOTA** (*Commelinaceae*)
　**elizabethae** (W. Equatorial Africa); ornamental leafy rosette, stalked foliage rich green w. yellow center band; white flower.　　　　p. 131

**PANDANUS** (*Pandanaceae*)
　**baptistii** (New Britain Is.) the "Blue screw-pine"; symmetrical with channeled leaves spirally arranged, blue green w. yellow center stripes.　　　　p. 82
　**utilis** (*Madagascar*), a large "Screw-pine", with leathery leaves keeled beneath, deep olive green but thorny with showy red spines.　　　　p. 82
　**veitchii** (Polynesia), "Variegated screw-pine"; attractive house plant; bold, spready rosette of leathery leaves shining green, lined and margined white.　　　　p. 82

**PAPHIOPEDILUM** (*Orchidaceae*)
　**callosum splendens** (Cambodia, Vietnam); vigorous terrestrial with marbled leaves, and elegant 10 cm flowers greenish and mahogany; beautiful top sepal striped cream and crimson.　　　　p. 61
　**godefroyae** (Burma to Vietnam); charming small terrestrial, with checkered leaves, the waxy 6—8 cm flowers white spotted crimson.　　　　p. 61
　**insigne** (Himalayas), in hort. as Cypripedium, a popular "Lady slipper"; terrestrial with plain green leaves, and glossy, waxy, 8—10 cm flowers white, yellow-green, purple; brown pouch.　　　　p. 61
　**x maudiae;** most beautiful with leaves marbled bluish and yellow; exquisite flowers in shades of white and green; excellent house plant.　　　　p. 61
　**rothschildianum** (Papua); remarkable, strong-growing, with striking flowers yellowish with purple, tail-like petals, and red-brown pouch.　　　　p. 61

**PARODIA** (*Cactaceae*)
　**sanguiniflora violacea** (Argentina), "Tom thumb cactus"; little 5 cm soft-green, spine-covered silky flowers red-violet; favorite window-sill plant very willing to bloom at young stage.　　　　p. 139

**PASSIFLORA** (*Passifloraceae*)
　**x alato-caerulea,** "Showy passion flower"; popular free-blooming hybrid with showy 10 cm fragrant flowers white and blue.　　　　p. 127
　**caerulea** (Brazil), a typical "Passion flower" with intriguing 9 cm flowers of greenish-white petal lobes and blue, white and purple corona.　　　　p. 127
　**coccinea** (Trop. So. America), "Scarlet passion flower", free-blooming with flowers glowing scarlet and yellow outside, the crown purple to white.　　　　p. 127
　**coriacea** (So. Mexico to Peru), known as "Bat-leaf"; with transverse butterfly leaves blue-green blotched with silver; small 3 cm fl. green and chocolate.　　　　p. 127
　**edulis** (Brazil), "Purple granadilla"; sturdy climber with 6 cm white flowers, followed by aromatic, edible fruit thickly dotted purple and quite ornamental.　　　　p. 71
　**incarnata** (Virginia to Texas), "Wild passion flower"; trilobed leaves and 5 cm flowers lavender and white, purplish filaments; edible yellow fruit.　　　　p. 127
　**maculifolia** (Venezuela), "Blotched-leaf passion vine"; fancy triangular foliage green marbled with yellow, purple beneath; flower white.　　　　p. 127
　**quadrangularis** (Trop. America), "Granadilla"; grown for its edible 12—25 cm fruit; fragrant red, white fl.　p. 127
　**racemosa** (Brazil), "Red passion flower"; a red-flowered passion vine, climbing by tendrils; 10 cm flowers, rosy-crimson, the fringed crown purple, tipped white. p. 127
　**trifasciata** (Venezuela to Peru), "Three-banded passion vine"; ornamental foliage beautifully colored satiny olive to bronze, with 3 broad pink to silver zones, purple beneath; small yellow flower.　　　　p. 127

**PAVONIA** (*Malvaceae*)
　**intermedia rosea** hort. (Brazil); stiffish shrub with terminal clusters of rosy flowers having prominent long stamens and bluish anthers.　　　　p. 65

**PELARGONIUM** (*Geraniaceae*)
　**capitatum 'Attar of Roses';** strongly rose-scented, foliage light green with slightly hairy surface; flower orchid pink.　　　　p. 32
　**denticulatum** (So. Africa), "Pine geranium"; pine-scented; clammy stems and dark green skeleton leaves; pinkish flower veined crimson.　　　　p. 32
　**denticulatum filicifolium,** "Fernleaf geranium"; pungent-scented, reminiscent of pine; fern-like green leafblades finely cut.　　　　p. 32

**x domesticum 'Earliana',** a charming "Pansy geranium" or "Regal geranium"; dwarf form with 3 cm leaves; flowers mainly orchid-colored, upper petals maroon.　　　　p. 26
　**x fragrans,** "Nutmeg geranium"; nutmeg-scented; small rounded and ruffled, grayish, soft-hairy leaves; small white flower marked purple.　　　　p. 32
　**graveolens** (So. Africa), the old-fashioned "Rose geranium"; old favorite house plant with sweetly rose-scented leaves, grayish with soft white hair; flowers lavender marked purple.　　　　p. 32
　**graveolens 'Minor',** "Little-leaf rose"; smaller leaves than the species above; fl. lavender rose with crimson. p. 32
　**graveolens 'Variegatum',** "Mint-scented rose-geranium"; grayish green, rough leaves edged in white, fragrant of roses with overtone of mint.　　　　p. 32
　**grossularioides** hort. (So. Africa), "Gooseberry geranium"; coconut-scented; small round, glossy leaves with scalloped margin like gooseberry; rosy flower. p. 32
　**x hortorum 'Antares';** spectacular miniature geranium w. dark foliage, and large flower dark scarlet.　　p. 31
　**x hortorum 'Irene';** popular commercial variety almost everblooming with large flowers cherry-red.　　p. 31
　**x hortorum 'Miss Burdett Coutts',** "Tricolor geranium"; most colorful leaves gray-green, ivory, pink and blood-red; single scarlet flower.　　　　p. 31
　**x hortorum 'Pygmy';** distinctive miniature with 2 cm leaves, vivid red flower.　　　　p. 31
　**x hortorum 'Wilhelm Langguth';** glistening grayish leaves bordered white; cherry-red flower.　　p. 31
　**x limoneum,** "Lemon geranium"; small lemon-scented three-lobed leaves; flower crimson-rose.　　p. 32
　**'M. Ninon',** "Apricot geranium"; apricot-scented coarse leaves deeply lobed; pink flower.　　　　p. 32
　**x nervosum,** "Lime geranium"; small 4 cm leaves, lime-scented; lavender flowers.　　　　p. 32
　**odoratissimum** (So. Africa), "Apple geranium"; ruffled moss-green silky leaves, small white fl. spotted red. p. 32
　**peltatum** (So. Africa), "Ivy geranium"; with ivy-like, fresh green waxy foliage; flower rose-carmine, also red, white or lavender.　　　　p. 31
　**peltatum 'L'Elegante',** "Sunset ivy geranium"; succulent gray green leaves edged in white and pink; small white flowers. Attractive in hanging baskets.　　p. 31
　**'Prince of Orange'** (citriodorum), "Orange geranium"; light green leaves with scent of orange peel; flower white w. purple.　　　　p. 32
　**'Prince Rupert';** lemon scented small, crinkly lobed leaves; flower lavender.　　　　p. 32
　**'Prince Rupert variegated',** also known as "French lace"; small lemon-scented foliage light green prettily edged in white.　　　　p. 32
　**quercifolium 'Fair Ellen',** "Oakleaf geranium"; lobed leaves with dark zoning; flower magenta pink.　p. 32
　**tomentosum** (So. Africa), "Peppermint geranium"; strongly mint-scented with large, velvety emerald green leaves; fluffy white flowers.　　　　p. 32
　**'Toronto',** "Ginger geranium"; sweetly ginger-scented, light green leaves; flower rosy-lavender.　　p. 32

**PELLAEA** (*Filices*)
　**rotundifolia** (New Zealand), "Button fern"; low miniature; long narrow fronds near the ground, with leaflets round when young, leathery dark green.　　　　p. 106
　**viridis** (hastata in hort.) (Madagascar), "Green cliff-brake"; tufted fern with lacy fronds on black stems.　p. 106
　**viridis macrophylla,** in hort. as "Pteris adiantoides"; divided fronds similar to holly fern but not as leathery. p. 106

**PELLIONIA** (*Urticaceae*)
　**daveauana** (South Vietnam), "Watermelon begonia"; succulent pinkish stems, and fleshy leaves brown purple with pale green center area.　　　　p. 129
　**pulchra** (South Vietnam), "Satin pellionia"; fleshy creeper with shingled leaves green to grayish, covered with network of brown veins.　　　　p. 129

**PENTAS** (*Rubiaceae*)
　**lanceolata** (Trop. Africa), "Egyptian star-cluster"; flowering plant with green, hairy leaves, and clusters of rosy blooms; also other colors.　　　　p. 62

**PEPEROMIA** (*Piperaceae*)
　**caperata** (Brazil), "Emerald ripple"; little rosette of roundish 4—6 cm quilted leaves, waxy forest green, on pink petioles. Flowering catkins greenish-white.　　p. 9, 119
　**clusiaefolia** (W. Indies), "Red-edged peperomia"; thick-fleshy, olive green leaves with purple margins.　p. 119
　**griseo-argentea;** in Brazil and Europe as hederaefolia, the "ivy peperomia"; shield-like quilted leaves painted silver. Somewhat particular.　　　　p. 119

**maculosa** (Santo Domingo), "Radiator plant"; fleshy leaves to 18 cm long, bluish gray-green, with silvery to ivory ribs. One of the largest species. p. 119

**marmorata** (So. Brazil), "Silver heart"; attractive with thin, heart-shaped leaves bluish green painted silver. p. 119

**obtusifolia** (Venezuela), "Baby rubber plant" or "Pepper face"; succulent with waxy, rich green 5–8 cm leaves. p. 119

**obtusifolia variegata**, "Variegated peperomia"; beautiful succulent plant with leaves milky green and creamy white; for dishgardens. p. 3

**polybotrya** (Colombia), "Coin leaf peperomia"; succulent with fleshy stem, supporting shield-like leaves of vivid green; white catkins. p. 119

**sandersii** (Brazil), "Watermelon peperomia"; beautiful rosette with red petioles bearing fleshy bluish leaves patterned with silver. p. 119

**scandens 'Variegata'** (Peru), "Variegated philodendron leaf"; fleshy pink-stemmed creeper with light to milky green leaves bordered white. p. 133

**verschaffeltii** (Brazil), "Sweetheart peperomia"; beautiful plant which I discovered on the upper Amazon; heart-shaped bluish leaves with silver bands. p. 5, 119

**PERESKIA** (*Cactaceae*)

**grandifolia** (Brazil), "Rose cactus"; characteristic of the most primitive of cacti having leaves; these are waxy green; rosy flowers looking like wild roses. p. 142

**PERISTROPHE** (*Acanthaceae*)

**angustifolia aureo-variegata** (Java), "Marble-leaf"; soft tropical herb with fresh-green leaves variegated rich yellow; small rosy flowers in terminal clusters. p. 121

**PETUNIA** (*Solanaceae*)

**x hybrida 'California Giant'**, "Giant pot petunia"; small herbaceous leaves dwarfed by giant 10–15 cm ruffled flowers in various colors. p. 25

**PHAIUS** (*Orchidaceae*)

**wallichii** (S.E. Asia), "Nun orchid"; majestic terrestrial with plaited leaves, and spike of fleshy, fragrant flowers brown, white, orange and red. p. 60

**PHALAENOPSIS** (*Orchidaceae*)

**amabilis 'Summit Snow'**, a "Moth orchid"; excellent hybrid with sprays of large 12 cm glistening white flowers. The species amabilis grows epiphytic in Indonesia. p. 60

**PHILODENDRON** (*Araceae*)

**andreanum** (Colombia), "Velour philodendron"; beautiful climber; iridescent velvety, dark olive leaves with ivory veins; translucent edge p. 91

**x barryi** (selloum x bipinnatifidum); vigorous decorative selfheader; large glossy foliage with broad segments. p. 88

**bipinnatifidum** (Brazil), an elegant "Tree-philodendron"; showy rosette forming trunk; waxy green, stiff leaves to 1 m long, with narrow segments. p. 88

**x 'Burgundy';** fine commercial hybrid slowly climbing, leathery 30 cm reddish leaves; young growth red. p. 91

**cannifolium** (Guyana), "Flask philodendron"; curious epiphyte with leathery leaves on swollen leafstalks. p. 90

**x corsinianum**, "Bronze shield"; gorgeous broad, quilted leaves coppery green with sinuate edge. p. 90

**domesticum,** in hort. as **hastatum** (Brazil), "Elephant's-ear"; lush climber with shining fresh green 30 cm leaves; inflorescence with tubular green spathe red inside. p. 89

**eichleri** (Brazil), "King of Tree-philodendrons"; magnificent leaves to 2 m long, metallic glossy green with scalloped margins. p. 88

**elegans** (Trop. So. America); high climber, with elegant thin-leathery deep gr. leaves, finger-like segments. p. 9, 90

**erubescens** (Colombia), "Blushing philodendron"; clamberer with 30 cm waxy leaves bronzy green edged red, wine-red beneath. p. 89

**x 'Florida'** (laciniatum x squamiferum), attractive with warty petioles carrying deep green leaves cut into 5 main-lobes. p. 89

**gloriosum** (Colombia), "Satin-leaf"; exquisite satiny leaves a beautiful silver green, with contrasting pinkish to white veins. p. 91

**grazielae** (fibrillosum) (Ecuador); charming dwarf climber with thick waxy heart-shaped, dark leaves. p. 89

**ilsemannii** (Brazil); spectacular climber with leathery leaves almost entirely white. p. 5, 91

**lacerum** (Cuba, Haiti); bold climber with mature leaves deeply incised, glossy green. p. 90

**lundii 'Sao Paulo'** (Brazil); tree-type; large, rich green foliage with segments elaborately frilled. p. 88

**x 'Lynette'**, the "Quilted birdsnest"; unusually attractive rosette, leathery quilted, fresh green leaves. p. 9

**mamei** (Ecuador), "Quilted silver leaf"; slow climber with waxy, corrugated leaves grayish, marbled with silver. p. 91

**x mandaianum** (domesticum x erubescens), "Red-leaf philodendron"; attractive arrow-shaped leaves and stems lacquered deep wine-red. p. 89

**melanochrysum** (Colombia, Costa Rica), "Black Gold"; beautiful but delicate; velvety black-olive leaves shimmering with pink, and pinkish veins. p. 91

**melinonii** (Surinam), "Red birdsnest"; magnificent rosette of broad leaves, red of sunlight, with pale veins, on red, swollen stalks. p. 90

**micans** (Tobago), "Velvet-leaf-vine"; leggy vine with small leaves glittering silky bronze, reddish beneath. p. 91

**microstictum** (pittieri) (Costa Rica); slow climber, with large and pleasing heart shaped, thick and glossy apple-green leaves. p. 89

**oxycardium** (Puerto Rico to Jamaica and C. America), known in horticulture as P. **cordatum,** the "Heartleaf philodendron" or "Parlor ivy"; most popular vining philodendron; rapid climber with glossy deep green heartshaped 10–15 cm leaves in juv. stage; in fl. stage to 30 cm. p. 89

**panduraeforme** (So. Brazil), "Fiddle-leaf", "Horse-head" or "Panda"; handsome climber with unusual olive green leaves fiddle-shaped. p. 89

**"pertusum"** as known in horticulture, actually the juvenile stage of *Monstera deliciosa*. Very popular decorator plant known as "Splitleaf", "Hurricane plant", or "Splitleaf philodendron". This young stage is more vining, the glossy green leaves are smaller, less incised and with fewer perforations. p. 87

**radiatum** (Mexico, Guatemala), in juvenile, less incised stage known as **P. dubia;** lush climber with broad rich green leaves deeply lobed. p. 90

**selloum** (S.W. Brazil), "Lacy tree-philodendron"; magnificent decorator with large rosette of elegant, deeply lobed leaves glossy dark green, ½ to 1 m across; ideal container plant where space permits. p. 14, 88

**sellowianum** (Brazil), fast growing self-header with large, deeply cut leaves which tolerate some cold. p. 88

**sodiroi** (Brazil), "Silver leaf philodendron"; beautiful with bluish-green leaves covered with silver, on wine-red petioles. p. 91

**squamiferum** (Guyana), "Red-bristle philodendron"; twisting vine with rich green 5-lobed leaves, ribs are red underneath; the petioles covered with red bristles. p. 9, 89

**verrucosum** (Costa Rica), "Velvet-leaf"; gorgeous, undulate leaves shimmering velvety bronzy green, violet underneath; red petioles with green bristles. p. 91

**wendlandii** (Costa Rica), "Birdsnest philodendron"; self-heading rosette of thick, waxy green leaves. p. 90

**PHLOX** (*Polemoniaceae*)

**drummondii** (Texas), "Dwarf annual phlox"; pretty little window-sill plant 15–20 cm high, in a riot of gay colors; clusters of 3 cm flowers rose, red, purple, blue, buff, or white. Lovely Mothers Day gift plant. p. 30

**PHOENIX** (*Palmae*)

**canariensis** (Canary Islands), "Canary date palm"; formal, massive palm with stiff fronds of pleated, glossy green leaflets. p. 101

**roebelenii** (Burma), "Pigmy date" or "Dwarf date palm"; graceful in tubs or as miniature in pots; globular crown with arching feathery fronds dark green and glossy. p. 101

**PHORMIUM** (*Liliaceae*)

**tenax 'Variegatum'** (New Zealand), "Variegated New Zealand flax"; decorative as tub plant; 2-ranked, tough leathery leaves brownish-green, margined cream and with red edges. p. 85

**PHRAGMIPEDIUM** (*Orchidaceae*)

**caudatum** (syn. Selenipedium) (Mexico to Peru), "Mandarin orchid"; sensational species with lush green leaves, and remarkable slipper flowers, with pendulous ribbon-like petals to 75 cm long, bronzy, yellowish and crimson. p. 60

**PHYLLITIS** (*Filices*)

**scolopendrium** (Intercontinental), "Hart's-tongue fern"; hardy fern with stout rhizome and long 15–45 cm straight leathery fronds bright green, undulate at margins. p. 112

**PILEA** (*Urticaceae*)

**cadierei** (Vietnam), "Aluminum plant" or "Watermelon pilea"; small, pretty foliage plant, with thin-fleshy 8 cm quilted bluish leaves, painted shining silvery. p. 21, 121

**involucrata** (spruceana) (Peru), "Friendship plant" or "Panamiga"; small ornamental with deeply quilted, hairy leaves coppery red-brown, wine-red beneath; tiny rose flowers. Considered a good house plant. p. 120

**microphylla** (muscosa) (West Indies), "Artillery plant"; popular little branching plant with fleshy stems, dense with tiny ½ cm watery-succulent green leaves. p. 132

**'Moon Valley'** hort. (So. Costa Rica) 1500 m, splendid foliage plant with square stems, fleshy 10 cm leaves deeply quilted, apple green with center and vein areas brown, covered with white bristles; clusters of tiny pinkish fl. p. 120

**nummularifolia** (W. Indies to Peru), "Creeping Charlie"; thin reddish branches with small quilted 2 cm hairy leaves light green. p. 132

**sp. 'Silver Tree'** hort. (Caribbean), "Silver and bronze"; densely branching little herb with quilted but glossy 3–8 cm bronzy leaves, broad silver band along center. p. 121

**PINUS** (*Pinaceae*)

**densiflora** (Japan), "Japanese red pine"; employed for miniature bonsai; slender blue green needles in pairs. p. 104

**mugo mughus** (Eastern Alps), "Dwarf Swiss mountain pine" or "Mugho pine"; shrubby little pine with twisted dark green needles in bundles of two; used in containers and for bonsai. p. 104

**nigra** (Austria to W. Asia), "Austrian pine"; long stiff, rigid needles green, in pairs; adaptable for bonsai. p. 104

**parviflora** (pentaphylla) (Japan, Taiwan), "Japanese white pine"; widely used in Japan for the culture of dwarfed bonsai in containers; bluish needles in clusters of five. p. 104

**thunbergii** (Japan), "Japanese black pine"; handsome tree with dark green, sharp-pointed stiff needles in pairs. Used for grafting of P. parviflora. p. 104

**PIPER** (*Piperaceae*)

**nigrum** (India to Java), "Black pepper"; tropical climber, dense with leathery blackish green 8–15 cm leaves; with age bearing clusters of red to black berries, furnishing black pepper. p. 128

**ornatum** (Celebes), "Celebes pepper"; exquisite climber with reddish stems, and shield-like 8–10 cm leaves green, traced with silvery pink. p. 128

**porphyrophyllum** (Indonesia), "Velvet cissus"; beautiful climber, with 8–10 cm leaves velvety moss green, yellow veins and pink markings, red underneath. p. 5

**PITTOSPORUM** (*Pittosporaceae*)

**tobira** (China, Japan), "Mock-orange" or "Australian laurel"; tough and handsome evergreen, with leathery, lustrous green 5–10 cm leaves; small creamy flowers fragrant as orange blossoms; durable tub plant. p. 77

**PLATYCERIUM** (*Filices*)

**bifurcatum** (E. Australia), "Staghorn fern"; curious epiphyte with kidney-shaped basal, sterile fronds; and pendant grayish, forked fertile fronds; easiest for home culture, tolerating some neglect. p. 109

**coronarium** (Malaya), "Crown staghorn"; glorious epiphyte with barren fronds tall and lobed; fresh green pendant fronds several times forked. Spore is carried on a separate disk. p. 109

**wilhelminae-reginae** (wandae), (New Guinea), "Queen elkhorn"; magnificent, with large crown of feathered sterile fronds; the glossy green pendant fronds in pairs, flanked on both outsides by triangular spore blades. p. 109

**willinckii** (Java), "Silver staghorn fern"; attractive with forked basal leaves, and very narrow, densely silvery-downy fertile fronds. p. 109

**PLECTRANTHUS** (*Labiatae*)

**australis** (Australia, Pacific Is.), "Swedish ivy", in California nurseries as "Creeping Charlie"; waxy 3–10 cm leaves metallic green; small white 2-lipped flowers in spikes. Good for hanging pots. p. 129

**coleoides 'Marginatus'** (So. India), "Candle plant"; charming foliage plant with hairy, grayish leaves and white margins; flower white with purple. p. 129

**oertendahlii** (Natal), "Prostrate coleus"; low, fleshy creeper, with 4 cm leaves friendly green to bronze, patterned with silver veins, purplish beneath; pink flower. p. 129

**purpuratus** (So. Africa), "Moth king"; wiry creeper; small silver-netted leaves, covered with velvety hairs; purplish beneath. p. 129

**PLEIOSPILOS** (*Aizoaceae*)

**bolusii** (So. Africa), "Living rock cactus"; stemless succulent with pairs of stone-like leaves gray green; yellow flower. p. 146

**nelii** (Cape Prov.), "Cleft stone"; a "Mimicry plant" in form of a split globe, gray with raised dark dots. p. 146

**simulans** (So. Africa), "African living rock"; small succulent, with pairs of triangular bronzy leaves 6–8 cm long; fragrant yellow flower. p. 150

**PLEOMELE** (*Liliaceae*)

**reflexa variegata** (So. India, Ceylon), "Song of India"; a beauty I first saw in Ceylon; slender flexuous stems, dense with clasping green leaves, beautifully margined golden cream. Very slow growing. p. 5, 80

**thalioides** (Trop. Africa), "Lance dracaena"; unusual decorative plant with leathery, glossy green lance-shaped leaves ribbed lengthwise. p. 81

**PLUMBAGO** (*Plumbaginaceae*)

**capensis (auriculata)** (So. Africa), "Blue Cape plumbago"; straggly plant with small foliage, and terminal clusters of light blue flowers. p. 68

**PLUMERIA** (*Apocynaceae*)

**rubra acutifolia** (Mexico), "Frangipani" or "Temple tree"; thick succulent branches with milky sap; long fleshy leaves and large 5–6 cm waxy-white flowers with yellow throat, and sweetly fragrant. p. 66

**PODOCARPUS** (*Podocarpaceae*)

**macrophyllus** (China, Japan), "Buddhist pine"; dense conifer with crowded leafy twigs; leathery dark green, needle-like foliage 5–12 cm long; bluish berries on female trees; male flowers resembling catkins. p. 103

**macrophyllus 'Maki'** (Japan), "Southern yew"; widely cultivated, and used as a tough, superb decorative container plant; more compact than species; smaller needles. p. 103

**Nagi** (Japan, Taiwan), "Broadleaf podocarpus"; handsome; spreading branches with broad, shining green, rigid-leathery 8 cm leaves; a durable display plant. p. 103

**POLIANTHES** (*Amaryllidaceae*)

**tuberosa** (Mexico), the well-beloved "Tuberose" of tropic countries; tuberous plant with leafy floral spikes, bearing the powerfully fragrant, waxy white flowers. p. 28

**POLYPODIUM** (*Filices*)

**aureum 'Undulatum'** (W. Indies, Brazil), "Blue fern" or "Hare's-foot fern"; creeping rhizomes, clothed with brown scales; wiry stalks bear exquisite wavy fronds, glaucous silvery blue. p. 108

**phyllitidis** (So. Florida, Brazil), "Strap fern"; from creeping rhizome rise strap-shaped fronds 25 to 75 cm long and 10 cm wide, glossy fresh green. p. 112

**polycarpon 'Grandiceps'** (Angola), "Fishtail fern"; curious house plant with thick-leathery, waxy yellow-green fronds, their tips forking to broad crests. p. 112

**subauriculatum** (Malaysia), "Pine fern"; elegantly decorative basket fern, with long pendant feathered fronds to 3 m long, glossy green. p. 110

**subauriculatum 'Knightiae'** (Australia), "Lacy pine fern"; beautiful, slow-growing basket fern with finely divided, lacy fronds. p. 110

**vulgare virginianum** (E. No. America to Labrador), the American "Wall fern"; hardy fern growing on rocks, by creeping rhizomes; the feathery fronds vivid green. p. 108

**POLYSCIAS** (*Araliaceae*)

**balfouriana** (New Caledonia), "Dinner plate aralia"; leafy shrub with willowy stems, large leathery leaves glossy green; first entire, later of 3 rounded leaflets. p. 74

**balfouriana marginata** (New Caledonia), "Variegated Balfour aralia"; variegated form, with the grayish-green leaflets having an irregular white border. p. 74

**balfouriana 'Pennockii'**, "White aralia"; attractive Puerto Rican cultivar, variegated and tinted creamy-white to pale green, dark green toward edge. p. 74

**filicifolia** (South Sea Islands), "Fernleaf aralia" or "Angelica"; flexuous stems, with fern-like leaves bright green, divided with leaflets cut into narrow lobes. p. 74

**fruticosa** (Malaysia), "Ming aralia"; a decorator's delight as tub plant; freely branching with willowy, twisting stems, and fern-like lacy, light green foliage. p. 73, 74

**fruticosa 'Elegans'** (Polynesia); compact form, dense with dark green leathery leaves, deeply cut into toothed lobes. Elegant small indoor plant. p. 74

**guilfoylei 'Quinquefolia'**, the "Celery-leaved panax"; selected Florida leaf form, with coppery leaves irregularly cut into 5 divisions or lobes. p. 74

**guilfoylei victoriae** (Polynesia), "Lace aralia"; charming with willowy branches, dense with lacy grayish green leaves, the feathery segments bordered white. p. 74

**paniculata 'Variegata'** (Mauritius), "Rose-leaf panax"; attractive willowy shrub, with divided leaves deep green and richly splashed with cream. p. 74

**POLYSTICHUM** (*Filices*)

**aristatum variegatum** (Japan to Australia), "East Indian holly-fern"; creeping rhizome bearing elegant leathery, divided fronds 30–60 cm long, the green segments banded pale yellow. p. 106

**tsus-simense** (Straits of Korea), in hort. as **Aspidium,** "Tsus-sima holly fern"; dwarf tufted fern for terrariums, with small leathery, dark green fronds to 20 cm long, lacily divided. Slow growing, good keeping quality. p. 106

**PORTULACARIA** (*Portulacaceae*)

**afra variegata** (So. Africa), "Rainbow bush" or "Elephant bush"; lovely little succulent with fleshy red stems, and tiny 2 cm leaves margined cream; red edge.          p. 147

**POTHOS** (*Araceae*)

**jambea** (Java); curious tree climber of the rainforest; the leaves with winged petiole, appearing as if constricted through the middle.          p. 129

**PRIMULA** (*Primulaceae*)

**obconica** (China), "German primrose"; cheerful winter-blooming pot-primrose with fresh green, strong-scented leaves, and clusters of showy 3–5 cm flowers in pastel shades of rose to almost blue.          p. 26

**PSEUDERANTHEMUM** (*Acanthaceae*)

**alatum** (Mexico), "Chocolate plant"; delicate but attractive copper-brown, papery leaves, silver-blotched near midrib; small purple flower.          p. 114

**atropurpureum tricolor** (Polynesia); colorful tropical shrubby plant, with small leathery leaves metallic purple, splashed green, white and pink.          p. 122

**reticulatum** (New Hebrides); attractive smooth foliage green with network of gold; wine-purple flowers          p.122

**PSEUDOPANAX** (*Araliaceae*)

**lessonii** (New Zealand), "False panax"; a tough decorator plant; slender stems with palmately compound shining green, leathery leaves, toothed toward apex.          p. 74

**PSEUDOSASA** (*Gramineae*)

**japonica** (Japan), "Metake bamboo" or "Female arrow bamboo"; running bamboo of moderate height, usually 2 m, with slender hollow stems and broad, persistent green foliage 10–30 cm long.          p. 83

**PSIDIUM** (*Myrtaceae*)

**cattleianum** (Brazil), "Strawberry guava"; dense shrub, with leathery green 5–8 cm leaves; white stamen flowers; and 4 cm edible red fruit.          p. 72

**PTERIS** (*Filices*)

**cretica 'Albo-lineata'**, "Variegated table fern"; pretty, variegated fern with small, clean cut leathery fronds with creamy-white bands.          p. 111

**cretica 'Rivertoniana'**, "Lacy table fern"; symmetrical form, with stiff erect fresh green fronds of firm texture, divided into deeply cut segments.          p. 111

**cretica 'Wilsonii'**, "Fan table fern"; excellent commercial low "Table fern" 15–20 cm high, the fresh green fronds forming fans at tips.          p. 111

**cretica 'Wimsettii'**, "Skeleton table fern"; robust variety, with leathery fronds divided into slender segments, irregularly lobed.          p. 111

**dentata** (Trop. and So. Africa), "Sleepy fern"; bushy, large fern with divided fronds to 1 m long, the deeply cut segments fresh green and somewhat soft.          p. 111

**ensiformis 'Victoriae'**, "Silver table fern"; beautiful little fern 15–35 cm, high with the leathery divided fronds prettily banded silvery-white, bordered in rich green. Ideal for terrariums.          p. 111

**multifida (serrulata)**, (Japan, China), "Chinese brake"; graceful, light green fronds, the segments are slender-narrow and distantly spaced.          p. 111

**quadriaurita 'Argyraea'** (C. India), "Silver bracken"; robust fern, with beautiful large fronds to 1 m high, segments deeply lobed, bluish-green with a center band of silvery white along the midrib.          p. 111

**quadriaurita 'Flabellata'** (So. Africa to Ethiopia), "Leather table fern"; elegant strong fern, with blackish stalks bearing pairs of glossy green segments.          p. 111

**semipinnata** (Hongkong, Philippines), "Angel-wing fern"; with fronds of distantly spaced segments which are deeply lobed on one side only.          p. 111

**tremula** (Tasmania, N.S. Wales), "Trembling brake fern"; robust grower with large bright green, herbaceous much divided fronds to 1 m tall.          p. 111

**vittata** (Old World tropics), in hort. as "longifolia"; rapid-growing with long arching feathered fronds, the segments dark green.          p. 111

**PTYCHOSPERMA** (*Palmae*)

**elegans** (Queensland), "Solitair palm" or "Princess palm"; handsome medium size feather palm to 7 m tall gracefully slender trunk topped by rather short fronds, the segment tips jagged as if cut off.          p. 99

**PUNICA** (*Punicaceae*)

**granatum legrellei** (S.E. Europe), "Double-flowering pomegranate"; free-blooming ornamental form of the pomegranate, showy 4 cm double flowers coral red.  p. 66

**granatum nana** (Iran to Himalayas), a dwarf "Pomegranate"; charming miniature for pot growing; shining green leaves, scarlet flowers; orange-red edible fruit.  p. 71

**PYRACANTHA** (*Rosaceae*)

**koidzumii 'Victory'** (of Taiwan origin), an excellent red "Fire-thorn"; thorny branches with deep green leathery foliage; small white, fragrant flowers; in winter with clusters of brilliant scarlet berries.          p. 69

**QUESNELIA** (*Bromeliaceae*)

**marmorata** (Brazil), "Grecian vase"; tall formal bluish tube, mottled green and maroon; pendant spike, rose bract leaves, blue flowers.          p. 42

**RAPHIOLEPIS** (*Roseceae*)

**indica 'Enchantress'** (origin China), "India hawthorn"; charming evergreen with leathery 8 cm leaves; large pretty flowers appleblossom-like rosy pink.          p. 66

**REBUTIA** (*Cactaceae*)

**kupperiana** (Bolivia), "Red crown cactus"; miniature spiny globe to 10 cm high; will bloom freely even as a tiny 3 cm plant, with showy scarlet flowers.          p. 136

**RECHSTEINERIA** (*Gesneriaceae*)

**cardinalis** (C. America), "Cardinal flower"; brilliantly flowered tuberous plant, with emerald green, velvety leaves, topped by curved tubular scarlet blooms.          p. 51

**leucotricha** (Brazil: Paraná), "Rainha do Abismo", or "Brazilian edelweiss", so named by me when I found it in Brazil because of its glistening silvery-hairy leaves, and slender tubular flowers soft coral; from huge tuber.          p. 51

**REINECKIA** (*Liliaceae*)

**carnea** (China), "Fan grass"; creeping rhizome, with thin-leathery, matte green leaves 1 cm wide; very durable.          p. 86

**RHAPHIDOPHORA** (*Araceae*)

**celatocaulis** (Borneo), "Shingle plant"; climber with fleshy leaves, in juvenile stage overlapping like shingles, and clinging close to tree or support.          p. 97

**decursiva** (Ceylon to Vietnam), stem stiffly climbing, large glossy green leaves divided to midrib.          p. 97

**RHAPIS** (*Palmae*)

**excelsa (flabelliformis)** (So. China), "Lady palm"; small fan palm, clustering with bamboo-like canes densely matted with coarse fiber; leathery, glossy green leaves w. 30 cm segments.          p. 14, 99

**RHEKTOPHYLLUM** (*Araceae*)

**mirabile** (Nephthytis picturata) (Nigeria); creeping, with large arrow-shaped leaves 30 cm or more, dark green variegated with silver.          p. 96

**RHIPSALIDOPSIS** (*Cactaceae*)

**gaertneri** (Schlumbergera) (So. Brazil), the epiphytic "Easter cactus"; flattened joints with scalloped purplish margins; starlike regular flowers deep scarlet.          p. 143

**x graeseri** (Epiphyllopsis); charming, free-blooming hybrid with small, wide open, star-shaped regular flowers rosy-red, in spring.          p. 143

**x graeseri 'Rosea'**; lovely epiphytic cactus with flowers clear pink, center flushed deep rose.          p. 143

**rosea** (Brazil: Paraná), "Dwarf Easter-cactus"; bushy with small 2 cm pencil-thin joints waxy green tinted purple; small 3 cm fl. rosy pink w. orchid edges.          p. 143

**RHIPSALIS** (*Cactaceae*)

**cassutha** (Florida to Brazil, Trop. Africa), "Mistletoe-cactus"; epiphytic, with light green branches thin-cylindrical, hanging in long strands; flower cream; mistletoe-like white berries.          p. 141

**RHOEO** (*Commelinaceae*)

**spathacea (discolor** in hort.) (Mexico, W. Indies), "Moses-in-the-cradle"; attractive rosette, of fleshy, waxy 20–30 cm leaves metallic dark green, purple beneath; in leaf bases little white flowers from shell-shaped bracts.          p. 131

**RHOICISSUS** (*Vitaceae*)

**capensis** (So. Africa), "Evergreen grape"; sturdy clambering vine from tubers; leathery glossy green 20 cm, leaves, rusty hairy beneath.          p. 128

**RHOMBOPHYLLUM** (*Aizoaceae*)

**dolabriforme** (So. Africa), "Hatchet plant"; curious succulent, with opposite hatchet-shaped 3–5 cm leaves, green w. translucent dots; yellow flowers.          p. 151

**nelii** (Hereroa in hort.) (So. Africa), "Elkhorns"; pale bluish-gray leaves 2-lobed at apex; 4 cm yellow fl.          p. 151

**ROHDEA** (*Liliaceae*)

**japonica** (Japan), "Sacred lily of China"; durable rosette, of thick-leathery matte-green leaves 5–8 cm wide; white flowers.          p. 82

**japonica marginata** (Japan), "Sacred Manchu lily"; rhizomatous fleshy rosette, with channeled leaves blackgreen, prettily bordered with white.          p. 86

**ROSA** (*Rosaceae*)

**chinensis minima** (roulettii) (China), "Pigmy rose"; well-loved miniature rose, averaging only 20–25 cm high; 4 cm double flowers lively rose-pink.          p. 66

**x grandiflora 'Queen Elizabeth'** (Hybrid tea x Floribunda); vigorous bush with tearose-type 9 cm, fragrant, soft pink flowers in clusters. p. 24

**x polyantha 'Margo Koster'**; excellent "Baby rose" of short compact habit, rather large globe-shaped flowers soft salmon. Good pot-forcer for Easter. p. 14, 17

**x polyantha 'Mother's-day'**; shapely "Polyantha rose" for pots; with glossy leaves, and clusters of crimson globular flowers in profusion. p. 24

**RUELLIA** (*Acanthaceae*)
**amoena** (So. America), "Redspray ruellia"; herbaceous shrub, with glossy green leaves; brilliant red 3 cm flowers streaked yellow. p. 68
**blumei** (Java); small herb, with stiff bluish green leaves marked silver, small bell-shaped flowers purplish. p. 122
**makoyana** (Brazil), "Monkey plant"; low herb, with small leaves satiny olive shaded violet, with silver veins; rosy flowers. p. 114

**RUMOHRA** (*Filices*)
**adiantiformis** (Polystichum coriaceum in hort.) (So. America to Polynesia), "Leather fern"; durable fresh green, leathery fronds lacily divided, from brown rhizome. p. 106

**SABAL** (*Palmae*)
**palmetto** (Carolina to Florida), "Cabbage palm" or "Palmetto"; fan palm with leaves 1–2 m long, divided into slender segments bluish above, gray underside. p. 102

**SAINTPAULIA** (*Gesneriaceae*)
**'Blue Boy-in-the-Snow'**, colorful sport of the early California ionantha-confusa hybrid Blue Boy 1930; foliage light green splashed cream; flowers violet-blue. p. 52
**confusa** (kewensis in hort.) (Tanzania), "Usambara violet"; miniature species with light green leaves, and medium-blue 3 cm flowers. p. 52
**'Diana'**; typical European cultivar of the vigorous Englert 'Harmonie' strain; rich green foliage, with full bouquet of large velvet purple flowers. p. 52
**diplotricha** (Tanzania); quilted, bronzy leaves, round 3 cm flowers lively sky-blue. p. 52
**ionantha** (Tanzania), the original "African violet"; parent of most present-day hybrids; found near sweltering Tanga 1892; large 2½–3 cm, pretty flowers light violet-blue, above coppery-green, pubescent leaves, red beneath. p. 52
**ionantha hybrid**, an "African violet" typical of many basic named hybrids or mutants of S. ionantha and confusa, with fl. in shades of violet to pink and white. p. 9
**'Kenya Violet'** (Roehrs 1964); vigorous hybrid, incorporating S. rupicola, which I found in Kenya, and producing long-lasting large 4–4½ cm double fl. violet-blue. p. 52
**'Rhapsodie Elfriede'**; typical cultivar of an excellent, prolific German strain with flowers of long lasting quality; 4 cm blooms intense dark blue, in formal mound above dark green foliage. p. 52
**rupicola** (S.E. Kenya); robust species which I found in 1960 high on bare rock north of Mombasa; prolific purplish-blue 2½–3 cm blooms; glossy green foliage. p. 52
**'Star Girl'**; typical of the "girl-type" scalloped leaves, with pale yellow center; white flowers edged in blue. p. 52

**SANCHEZIA** (*Acanthaceae*)
**nobilis glaucophylla** (Ecuador); handsome with soft-leathery 22 cm leaves, glossy green with yellow veins; large yellow flowers. p. 123

**SANSEVIERIA** (*Liliaceae*)
**cylindrica** (Natal), "Spear sansevieria"; rigid cylindric leaves 3 cm dia., usually grooved, dark green with gray cross-banding. p. 152
**ehrenbergii** (E. Africa), "Blue sansevieria" or "Seleb"; elegant with angular blue-green leaves, fan-like. p. 152
**grandis** (Somaliland), "Grand Somali hemp"; epiphytic succulent, with 15 cm broad leaves dull green, with bands of deeper green. p. 152
**intermedia** (E. Trop. Africa), "Pygmy bowstring"; dense rosette of thick, channeled, recurved gray-green leaves marked with pale cross-bands. p. 152
**"Kirkii"** hort. (Africa: Zaïre), "Star sansevieria"; starry rosette of narrow, angled leaves, dull grass-green cross-banded with gray. p. 152
**senegambica, cornui** in hort. (Senegal); broad leaves with concave margin, matte medium green. p. 152
**trifasciata 'Bantel's Sensation'**, "White sansevieria"; beautiful sport of laurentii; long slender leaves, with lengthwise bands of white, edged with green. p. 152
**trifasciata 'Hahnii'**, "Birdsnest sansevieria"; low, vase-like rosette, of broad leaves 10–15 cm long, dark green with pale cross bands. p. 146, 152
**trifasciata 'Golden hahnii'**, "Golden birdsnest"; very decorative succulent flattened rosette, grayish green with golden-yellow margins. p. 9, 152

**trifasciata laurentii** (Africa: Zaïre), "Variegated snake plant"; very satisfactory house plant, with stiff-erect, fleshy leaves deep green, with broad yellow bands along margins; small whitish fragrant flowers. p. 152
**zeylanica** (Ceylon), "Devil's tongue"; spreading rosette, of recurving fleshy leaves, grayish green with dark green crossbands. p. 152

**SARCOCOCCA** (*Buxaceae*)
**ruscifolia** (W. China), "Sweet box"; slow-growing evergreen; leathery 5–8 cm dark green leaves with wavy margins; small white fragrant flowers. p. 78

**SARRACENIA** (*Sarraceniaceae*)
**drummondii** (Georgia to Alabama), "Lace trumpets"; carnivorous "Pitcher plant" with tall fluted, fresh green tubes veined with purple; the lid marbled white. p. 120

**SAXIFRAGA** (*Saxifragaceae*)
**sarmentosa** (China, Japan), the "Strawberry geranium" or "Mother of thousands"; tufted perennial, sending out runners; bristly 3–5 cm leaves olive green with silver tracings, purple beneath; numerous white flowers. p. 129
**sarmentosa 'Tricolor'**, the "Magic carpet"; beautiful with leaves dark and milky green, variegated ivory and tinted pink. p. 121

**SCHIZOCENTRON** (*Melastomaceae*)
**elegans** (Mexico), "Spanish shawl"; basket plant, with reddish stems, small green leaves, and covered with purple 2½ cm flowers. p. 133

**SCHLUMBERGERA** (*Cactaceae*)
**bridgesii** (Bolivia?), "Christmas cactus"; epiphyte with glossy green, leaf-like joints; pendant fl. carmine-red. p. 143
**russelliana** (Brazil), "Shrimp cactus"; epiphyte with small scalloped joints, and star-shaped flowers orange red in spring. p. 143

**SCHOMBURGKIA** (*Orchidaceae*)
**undulata** (Trinidad to Colombia), bold epiphyte with tall, handsome cluster of waxy; 4 cm purple flowers and pink lip; blooming between December and July. p. 60

**SCILLA** (*Liliaceae*)
**peruviana** (Algeria), "Cuban lily"; handsome plant, with cluster of small, star-like lilac-blue flowers, above fresh green foliage. Not winter hardy. p. 28
**violacea** (So. Africa), "Silver squill"; attractive small suckering plant, with variegated 8–12 cm foliage olive green, painted silver, glossy red beneath. p. 122

**SCINDAPSUS** (*Araceae*)
**aureus** (Solomon Islands), "Devil's ivy", commercially known as "Pothos"; climbing by rootlets, with waxy foliage dark green, variegated yellow; popular house plant. p. 96
**aureus 'Marble Queen'**, "Taro-vine"; colorful mutant with green leaves richly variegated white. p. 5, 9, 96
**pictus** (Indonesia); tropical climber clinging to trees, leathery leaves green, overlaid with greenish silver. p. 96
**pictus argyraeus** (Borneo), "Satin pothos"; beautiful creeper, with smaller leaves satiny, bluish with silver. p. 96

**SCIRPUS** (*Cyperaceae*)
**cernuus** (Isolepis gracilis in hort.), "Miniature bulrush"; grass-like, tufted miniature, with numerous thread-like, glossy green leaves becoming pendant. p. 86

**x SEDEVERIA** (*Crassulaceae*)
**derenbergii** (Echeveria x Sedum), "Baby echeveria"; trim little rosette 4–5 cm dia., bluish gray. p. 148

**SEDUM** (*Crassulaceae*)
**adolphii** (Mexico), "Golden sedum"; small branching succulent, with boatshaped 3–4 cm leaves waxy yellow-green with reddish margins; white flowers. p. 147
**morganianum** (Mexico), "Burro tail"; lovely succulent, with pendant tassels dense with short leaves, glaucous silvery blue; flowers pink. p. 150
**rubrotinctum** (guatemalense in hort.) (Mexico), "Christmas cheers"; branching stem, with thickly clustered 2 cm club-shaped leaves, glossy green tipped brown. p. 147

**SELAGINELLA** (*Selaginellaceae*)
**caulescens** (Sunda Islands), "Stalked selaginella"; erect wiry stalks, with firm, lacy fronds bright green. p. 113
**emmeliana** (So. America), "Sweat plant"; tufted small rosette, with lacy foliage bright green, usually 8–15 cm high, revelling in high humidity. p. 113
**kraussiana**, in hort. as **denticulata** (Cameroons), "Club moss" or "Trailing Irish moss"; charming mat-forming delicate herb, with tiny crowded, bright green leaves. p. 113
**kraussiana browni** (Azores), "Cushion moss" or "Irish moss"; shapely, moss-like mounds vivid emerald green; pretty in terrariums. p. 3, 113
**martensii divaricata** (Mexico), "Zigzag selaginella"; erect branched zigzag stems, with vivid glossy green, hard, finely cut leaves. p. 113

**willdenovii** (Vietnam), "Peacock fern"; strikingly beautiful tall-climbing, with spreading fronds of shimmering peacock-blue.                                                         p. 113

**SELENICEREUS** (*Cactaceae*)

**grandiflorus** (Jamaica), the best known "Queen of the Night"; climbing epiphyte, with large nocturnal flowers salmon outside, white inside, perfumed vanilla.           p. 142

**SEMPERVIVUM** (*Crassulaceae*)

**tectorum calcareum** (Alps), "Houseleek" or "Hen-and-chickens"; clustering 8–10 cm rosettes, gray green with brown tips; for dishgardens.                           p. 147

**SENECIO** (*Compositae*)

**cineraria 'Diamond'** (Mediterranean), "Dusty miller"; beautiful snow-white woolly perennial, with feathered leaves; flowers yellow.                                    p. 30

**cruentus 'Multiflora nana'**, "Cineraria" of florists; bushy herbaceous potplant, with soft-fleshy leaves; showy clusters of white-eyed, 4 cm flowers in many colors, pink, red to blue.                                             p. 24

**jacobsenii** (Kenya), "Weeping notonia"; creeping succulent, with fleshy 8 cm leaves glossy green; flowers orange. For sunny windows and hanging pots.        p. 150

**macroglossus variegata**: (Kenya), "Variegated wax-ivy"; attractive rambling succulent with 3–4 cm ivy-like, but fleshy leaves, milky green bordered cream.            p. 150

**mikanioides** (So. Africa), "Parlor ivy" or "German ivy"; herbaceous rambler, with fresh-green ivy-shaped leaves; fragrant yellow disk flowers.                  p. 129

**serpens**, better known as **Kleinia repens** (So. Africa), "Blue chalk sticks"; low succulent, with fleshy, cylindrical leaves waxy bluish gray.                            p. 146

**SETCREASEA** (*Commelinaceae*)

**purpurea** (Mexico), "Purple heart"; so named because of the striking purple color of this rambling downy creeper; flower lilac.                                 p. 130

**SIDERASIS** (*Commelinaceae*)

**fuscata** (Brazil), "Brown spiderwort"; pretty rosette of 20 cm olive green leaves, with silver center band, covered by brown hair; flowers blue.                           p. 131

**SINNINGIA** (*Gesneriaceae*)

**pusilla** (Brazil), "Miniature slipper plant"; darling little rosette, of olive green 1 cm leaves and exquisite purple flowers 1½ cm across. Best grown in a glass brandy-snifter.                                            p. 51

**regina** (Brazil), "Cinderella slippers"; beautiful, compact species, with large velvety, bronzy leaves prettily patterned with ivory veins; nodding violet flowers.         p. 5, 51

**speciosa** (Brazil), "Violet slipper gloxinia"; compact tuberous species, with white-velvety leaves, and showy flowers to 5 cm long, usually violet blue.            p. 51

**speciosa 'Emperor Frederick'**, the "Gloxinia" of florists; favorite commercial hybrid, with large velvety leaves; upright bell flowers to 10 cm across, velvety crimson bordered white.                                     p. 15

**SKIMMIA** (*Rutaceae*)

**japonica 'Nana'** (Japan), "Dwarf Japanese skimmia"; handsome low evergreen, with leathery, glossy green 6 cm leaves, fragrant white flowers; female plants with coral berries. Long lasting decorative fruiting plant.        p. 72

**SMITHIANTHA** (*Gesneriaceae*)

**zebrina** (Naegelia) (Mexico), "Temple bells"; gorgeous silky-hairy species, leaves with red tracery; the 4 cm bells scarlet with yellow, in spires.                       p. 51

**SOLANUM** (*Solanaceae*)

**pseudo-capsicum** (Madeira), "Jerusalem cherry" or "Christmas cherry"; popular old houseplant, dense with silky leaves; the small white star-flowers followed by lustrous orange-scarlet 2½ cm berries in winter.      p. 69

**SONERILA** (*Melastomaceae*)

**margaritacea 'Mme. Baextele'** (Java), "Frosted sonerila"; exquisite miniature, with silvery, bristly foliage, puckered with pearly spots.                          p. 114

**SPARMANNIA** (*Tiliaceae*)

**africana** (So. Africa), "Indoor-linden"; an old house plant, with light green white-hairy 15–25 cm leaves.  p. 79

**SPATHICARPA** (*Araceae*)

**sagittifolia** (Brazil), "Fruit-sheath plant"; conversation plant, with inflorescence bearing tiny male and female flowers, attached along recurved green spathe.      p. 98

**SPATHIPHYLLUM** (*Araceae*)

**'Clevelandii'**, "White flag" or "Peace lily"; excellent decorator plant; handsome with glossy-green leaves, freely blooming with large 10–15 cm white spathes.       p. 92

**floribundum** (Colombia), "Spathe flower"; dwarf plant, with satiny foliage; small 5–8 cm white spathe.   p. 9, 92

**STAPELIA** (*Asclepiadaceae*)

**gigantea** (Zululand), "Giant toad plant" or "Zulu giants"; clustering, velvety stems producing gigantic star-shaped, 25–40 cm yellow flowers lined crimson, unfortunately with unpleasant odor.                                  p. 151

**hirsuta** (So. Africa), "Hairy toad plant"; stubby, clustering hairy fingers sooty green; 10–12 cm flowers cream lined purple. Of compact size; a favorite dishgarden plant.  p. 146

**variegata** (So. Africa), "Carrion flower" or "Spotted toad cactus"; soft-fleshy stems mottled purple; showy greenish 5–8 cm flowers with purple spots.        p. 151

**STENANDRIUM** (*Acanthaceae*)

**lindenii** (Peru), attractive tropical herb; the metallic coppery leaves with yellow veins; flowers yellow.   p. 114

**STENOCHLAENA** (*Filices*)

**palustris** (India to Australia), "Liane fern"; epiphytic climber, with leathery divided fronds shining green. p. 110

**STENOTAPHRUM** (*Gramineae*)

**secundatum variegatum** (Trop. America), the variegated "St. Augustine grass"; creeping grass, with firm leaves prettily banded white.                            p. 86

**STEPHANOTIS** (*Asclepiadaceae*)

**floribunda** (Madagascar), "Madagascar jasmine"; wiry climber with glossy green leaves; axillary clusters of exquisite waxy white, fragrant flowers 5 cm wide.        p. 126

**STRELITZIA** (*Musaceae*)

**reginae** (So. Africa), "Bird-of-paradise"; clustering, with stiff-leathery, bluish gray leaves; fantastic bird-like inflorescence with orange and blue flowers.              p. 63

**STREPTOCARPUS** (*Gesneriaceae*)

**x hybridus** (So. Africa), "Cape primrose"; long quilted, fleshy leaves; large trumpet flowers 8–10 cm dia., in colors white, rose to purple.                           p. 51

**STROBILANTHES** (*Acanthaceae*)

**dyerianus** (Burma), "Persian shield"; beautiful foliage plant, 15 cm leaves in iridescent purple with silver.    p. 123

**SYAGRUS** (*Palmae*)

**weddelliana**, in hort. as **Cocos weddelliana** (Brazil), "Terrarium palm"; charming little feather palm, glossy yellow-green; for terrariums.                       p. 102

**SYNGONIUM** (*Araceae*)

**podophyllum albolineatum** (Nicaragua), "Arrowhead vine"; very ornamental foliage, green with silver.       p. 97

**podophyllum 'Trileaf Wonder';** attractive with leaves highly painted with silvery green; in maturity stage leaves become divided.                                    p. 97

**podophyllum xanthophilum** (Mexico), cultivated as "Green Gold"; the juvenile arrow-shaped leaves marbled with yellow green; used for dishgardens.            p. 97

**wendlandii** (Costa Rica); dainty creeper; deep green, velvety leaves with vein areas white.              p. 5, 9

**TAVARESIA** (*Asclepiadaceae*)

**grandiflora** (S.W. Africa), "Thimble flower"; succulent green stems 20 cm high, with white-bristled ridges; flowers yellow spotted red.                              p. 151

**TETRAPANAX** (*Araliaceae*)

**papyriferus** (China), "Rice paper plant"; small tree, with 25 cm foliage gray green, white-felted beneath; creamy flowers.                                     p. 74

**THUNBERGIA** (*Acanthaceae*)

**alata** (S.E. Africa), "Black-eyed Susan"; twining herb, with showy flowers orange, with black-purple throat. p. 129

**THRINAX** (*Palmae*)

**parviflora** (Caribbean), "Florida thatch palm"; slender solitary fan palm, with fronds 1 m across, green on both sides. Shapely, attractive tub plant.            p. 102

**TIBOUCHINA** (*Melastomaceae*)

**semidecandra** (Brazil), "Glory bush" or "Princess flower"; showy flowering shrub, with fresh green velvety leaves; large 8 cm brilliant purple blossoms.        p. 68

**TILLANDSIA** (*Bromeliaceae*)

**fasciculata** (Florida to C. America), "Wild pine"; large epiphyte, with hard 45 cm gray leaves; branched inflorescence with reddish bracts, and blue flowers.         p. 48

**flexuosa** (Florida to S. America), "Spiralled airplant"; hard rosette, with leaves twisted, silvery gray; rosy bracts and white flowers.                            p. 48

**lindenii** (Peru), "Blue-flowered torch"; striking rosette of green leaves with red pencil lines; spike of flattened rosy bracts, with large blue flowers.                  p. 48

**usneoides** (New Jersey to Chile), the "Spanish moss"; true epiphyte, growing from trees; threadlike silvery masses, with tiny hidden flowers green or blue.         p. 48

**TITANOPSIS** (*Aizoaceae*)

**calcarea** (So. Africa), "Limestone mimicry"; clustering stemless, weird little gray, white-warted succulent, mimicking stones; flowers yellow.                       p. 146

**TOLMIEA** (*Saxifragaceae*)
   **menziesii** (Alaska, Brit. Columbia, Oregon), "Piggyback plant"; a curiosity plant, with bristly, fresh-green leaves, each of which can produce young plantlets from the base.  p. 134
**TRACHELOSPERMUM** (*Apocynaceae*)
   **jasminoides** (Himalayas), "Confederate jasmine"; small woody evergreen, slowly climbing; 5–8 cm leathery leaves; small white, very fragrant star-like flowers.  p. 126
**TRACHYCARPUS** ( *Palmae*)
   **fortunei,** grown as **Chamaerops excelsa** in hort. (Japan), the "Windmill palm"; fan palm, with trunk covered by brown fiber; shiny dark green fronds to 1 m dia. somewhat winter-hardy.  p. 102
**TRADESCANTIA** (*Commelinaceae*)
   **fluminensis 'Variegata'** (Argentina), "Variegated wandering Jew" or "Speedy Henry"; lively little creeper, with fresh green leaves, striped creamy white.  p. 130
   **sillamontana** (N.E. Mexico), introduced as "White velvet"; fleshy trailer, entirely covered with fluffy white wool; orchid flowers.  p. 130
**TRICHOCEREUS** (*Cactaceae*)
   **pachanoi** (Ecuador), "Night-blooming San Pedro"; slender, green column cactus; large white, nocturnal flowers very fragrant.  p. 137
**TRIFOLIUM** (*Leguminosae*)
   **repens minus** (Europe), "Irish shamrock"; dwarf form of the white clover, each leaf with 3 fresh green leaflets. Grown by florists in miniature pots, to honor St. Patrick. A favorite for St. Patrick's Day, March 17.  p. 124
**TULIPA** (*Liliaceae*)
   **'Red Giant';** a stocky, late Triumph tulip, grown for Easter, with long-lasting, firm scarlet flower.  p. 27
**TURNERA** (*Turneraceae*)
   **ulmifolia angustifolia** (W. Indies to Argentina), "West Indian holly"; herbaceous shrub, with glossy green leaves, and pretty, yellow 5 cm flowers.  p. 62
**URGINEA** (*Liliaceae*)
   **maritima** (Canary Isl. to Syria), "Sea onion"; large bulb; produces glaucous basal leaves; after wilting and resting the floral spike appears, bearing starry whitish flowers.  p. 29
**VANDA** (*Orchidaceae*)
   **coerulea** (Assam, Burma), the beautiful "Blue orchid"; stems with 2-ranked leaves; axillary inflorescence with exquisite flowers in shades of blue.  p. 61
   **x 'Miss Agnes Joaquim'** (Singapore), "Corsage orchid" or "Moon orchid"; prolific epiphyte with cylindric leaves, climbing, pencil-like stems, and large 7 cm blooms light purple, with darker lip.  p. 61
   **tricolor** (Java, Bali), beautiful "Strap vanda"; stems with 2 ranks of recurving strap leaves; waxy 5–7 cm flowers, yellow spotted red, lip white with purple, and fragrant. p. 61
**VANILLA** (*Orchidaceae*)
   **fragrans 'Marginata'** (E. Mexico), "Variegated vanilla"; striking epiphytic climber, with fleshy stem, the alternate leaves milky green with white margins.  p. 60
**VEITCHIA** (*Palmae*)
   **merrillii** (Philippines), "Christmas palm" or "Manila palm"; medium sized feather palm, with compact crown of green fronds, their tips jagged; lustrous red fruit.  p. 99
**VELTHEIMIA** (*Liliaceae*)
   **viridifolia** (So. Africa), "Forest-lily"; handsome bulbous rosette of lacquer green leaves; tall inflorescence of nodding 4 cm flowers, yellowish to dusty red.  p. 29
**VIBURNUM** (*Caprifoliaceae*)
   **suspensum** (Ryukyu Islands); handsome evergreen shrub, with dark green leathery leaves, and tiny white, fragrant flowers.  p. 66
**VINCA** (*Apocynaceae*)
   **major variegata** (So. Europe to Africa), "Band plant"; thin-wiry vines, with green waxy-glossy leaves 5 cm long, prettily edged cream; large blue flowers.  p. 132
**VRIESEA** (*Bromeliaceae*)
   **carinata** (S.E. Brazil), "Lobster claws"; dainty epiphyte, with pale green foliage; flattened spike with bracts yellow and crimson; flowers yellow.  p. 9
   **hieroglyphica** (Brazil), "King of bromeliads"; large regal, yellow-green rosette, fantastically cross-banded dark green to brown; flowers yellow.  p. 47
   **imperialis** (Brazil), "Giant vriesea"; gigantic terrestrial rosette of leathery leaves, turning wine-red in sun; inflorescence 2 m tall, with bracts maroon and yellow flowers.  p. 47
   **x mariae** (carinata hybrid), "Painted feather"; light green rosette; striking inflorescence feather-like, salmon rose to yellow, yellow flowers.  cover, 47

**x poelmannii,** vigorous, shapely light green rosette; inflorescence a branched spike of crimson-red bracts with greenish yellow apex; yellow flowers.  cover
   **splendens 'Major'** (Guyana), "Flaming sword"; spectacular bluish green rosette, marked with purple crossbands; long floral spike flat with scarlet bracts, yellow fl. p. 5, 47
**WEDELIA** (*Compositae*)
   **trilobata** (W. Indies); trailing herb, with fresh green 5–10 cm leaves, and attractive fl. golden yellow.  p. 133
**XANTHOSOMA** (*Araceae*)
   **lindenii 'Magnificum'** (Colombia), "Indian kale"; beautiful foliage plant, with deep green leaves, strikingly veined and margined white.  p. 3, 98
**YUCCA** (*Liliaceae*)
   **aloifolia 'Marginata'** (W. Indies, Mexico), "Spanish bayonet"; attractive stiff rosette of sharp-pointed, dagger-like leaves, 5 cm wide, glaucous with creamy margins. p. 85
   **elephantipes** (Mexico, Guatemala), "Spineless yucca"; a "Palm lily" with leafy trunk having swollen base; soft-leathery leaves to 8 cm wide, glossy grass-green, with rough margins and soft tip; cluster of ivory white flowers. p. 85
**ZAMIA** (*Cycadaceae*)
   **furfuracea** (Mexico to Colombia), "Jamaica sago-tree"; short trunk bearing handsome feathered leaves; the thick-leathery leaflets broad and metallic green.  p. 100
**ZANTEDESCHIA** (*Araceae*)
   **aethiopica** (So. Africa to Egypt), "Calla-lily"; robust marsh-loving herb, with thick rhizome; glossy green leaves, and large funnel shaped, waxy-white spathe; spadix yellow. For winter flowering must rest in summer.  p. 28
   **elliottiana** (So. Africa), "Yellow calla"; bright green leaves with translucent white spots; the flaring 15 cm spathe rich yellow.  p. 28
**ZEBRINA** (*Commelinaceae*)
   **pendula** (Mexico), "Silvery wandering Jew"; fleshy trailer, with 5 cm leaves deep green to purple, with two glistening silver bands; purple beneath; fl. purple.  p. 130
   **pendula 'Discolor',** "Tricolor wandering Jew"; glossy coppery and nile-green foliage, overlaid and edged metallic purple, and two silver bands.  p. 130
   **purpusii** (Mexico), "Bronze wandering Jew"; vigorous creeper, with shingled 5–6 cm leaves purplish brown; vivid purple beneath.  p. 130
**ZYGOCACTUS** (*Cactaceae*)
   **truncatus** (Brazil), "Thanksgiving cactus" or "Crab-cactus"; beautiful epiphyte; flat, glossy gree joints, with prominent teeth toward apex; irregular scarlet fl.  p. 143
   **truncatus delicatus,** "White crab-cactus"; long dark green joints sharply toothed; the irregular white flowers delicately tinged pink. November-December blooming.  p. 143
**ZYGOPETALUM** (*Orchidaceae*)
   **mackayi** (So. Brazil); striking robust orchid, with pseudo-bulbs bearing a fan of long leaves; floral stalk with beautiful waxy 5–7 cm flowers, yellow-green with purple, lip white veined blue; very fragrant.  p. 61

# Common Names
# of Exotic Plants

Some descriptive

"Sadsack"
*Mammillaria parkinsonii*

Some humorous

"Smiling Jack"
*Mammillaria nejapensis*

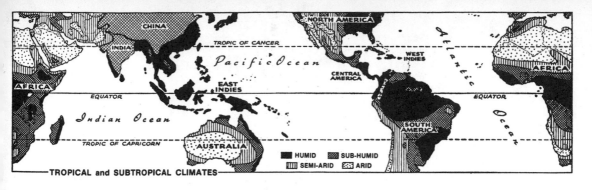

HUMID    SUB-HUMID
SEMI-ARID    ARID

—TROPICAL and SUBTROPICAL CLIMATES—

# PLANT GEOGRAPHY

To give a potential indoor plant the best possible chance of success, we should know something about the climatic backgrounds that prevail in their native habitats. Environment has shaped characteristics in plant types that make them either tolerant or difficult to acclimate when taken into cultivation. If too sensitive it may be best not to try them as a house plant, but many tropicals are far too beautiful not to tempt us to experiment with them just the same.

This is where knowledge of their origin helps us to provide for them those conditions under which such plants feel at home. Each climatic zone has favored and subsequently evolved plant populations that are peculiar to it.

As if by magic carpet, the fascinating world of the Collector of Exotics extending East from the tropics of the Western hemisphere to subtropical Europe, the vast expanse of Africa and Monsoon Asia and on to Australasia and the islands of the Southern Seas— these are the areas where our house plants were originally found.

*Temperature and Rainfall* at typical locations in the Tropic and Subtropic Zones.

| NORTH AMERICA | LAT. deg. | ELEV. feet | TEMP. °F. min. | TEMP. °F. max. | RAIN in. |
|---|---|---|---|---|---|
| California, San Diego | 32.7 N | 131 | 35 | 88 | 11 |
| Florida, Miami | 25.8 N | 10 | 27 | 95 | 56 |
| Mexico, Mexico City | 19.2 N | 7575 | 24 | 92 | 29 |
| Mexico, Vera Cruz | 19.1 N | 52 | 49 | 96 | 63 |
| **WEST INDIES** | | | | | |
| Cuba, Habana | 23.8 N | 161 | 50 | 95 | 48 |
| Puerto Rico, San Juan | 18.2 N | 100 | 62 | 94 | 61 |
| Jamaica, Kingston | 18.1 N | 24 | 57 | 98 | 33 |
| **CENTRAL AMERICA** | | | | | |
| Guatemala, Guatemala City | 14.3 N | 4855 | 41 | 90 | 51 |
| Costa Rica, San José | 9.5 N | 3760 | 47 | 94 | 71 |
| Panama, Colón | 9.2 N | 25 | 66 | 95 | 127 |
| **SOUTH AMERICA** | | | | | |
| Venezuela, Caracas | 10.3 N | 3420 | 45 | 91 | 32 |
| Venezuela, Ciudad Bolivar | 8.9 N | 125 | 66 | 97 | 35 |
| Guyana, Georgetown | 6.5 N | 70 | 68 | 92 | 90 |
| Colombia, Buenaventura | 3.5 N | 39 | 73 | 92 | 390 |
| Ecuador, Quito (Sierra) | 0.1 S | 9350 | 36 | 78 | 49 |
| Ecuador, Mendez (Oriente) | 2.4 S | 2290 | 61 | 89 | 102 |
| Brazil, Manaos (Amazonas) | 3.0 S | 147 | 66 | 101 | 72 |
| Brazil, Rio de Janeiro | 22.5 S | 210 | 52 | 102 | 43 |
| Brazil, Sao Paulo | 23.3 S | 2690 | 28 | 101 | 56 |
| Peru, Iquitos (Amazon) | 3.7 S | 295 | 64 | 88 | 103 |
| Peru, Lima | 12.3 S | 512 | 40 | 90 | 2 |
| Peru, Cuzco | 13.3 S | 11.319 | 28 | 80 | 32 |
| Bolivia, La Paz | 16.3 S | 12.001 | 27 | 75 | 22 |
| Chile, Santiago | 33.2 S | 1706 | 24 | 99 | 14 |
| Argentina, Buenos Aires | 34.3 S | 82 | 28 | 103 | 38 |
| **EUROPE** | | | | | |
| France, Marseilles | 43.1 N | 246 | 12 | 100 | 23 |
| Italy, Palermo (Sicily) | 38.1 N | 229 | 37 | 97 | 30 |
| Spain, Seville (Andalusia) | 37.2 N | 98 | 22 | 124 | 19 |

| AFRICA | LAT. deg. | ELEV. feet | TEMP. °F. min. | TEMP. °F. max. | RAIN in. |
|---|---|---|---|---|---|
| Egypt, Cairo | 30.3 N | 98 | 31 | 113 | 1 |
| Cameroon, Douala | 4.0 N | 33 | 66 | 90 | 156 |
| Equat. Africa, Brazzaville | 4.2 S | 951 | 53 | 101 | 49 |
| East Africa, Nairobi | 1.1 S | 5450 | 36 | 89 | 38 |
| Tanzania, Amani (Usamb.) | 4.5 S | 3100 | 45 | 86 | 50 |
| Tanzania, Tanga | 5.1 S | 98 | 64 | 93 | 61 |
| Madagascar, Tamatave | 18.9 S | 13 | 55 | 100 | 125 |
| So. Africa, Johannesburg | 26.1 S | 5750 | 23 | 90 | 33 |
| South Africa, Cape Town | 33.5 S | 40 | 31 | 104 | 25 |
| **ASIA** | | | | | |
| Israel, Haifa | 32.6 N | 33 | 35 | 99 | 27 |
| Japan, Nagasaki | 32.4 N | 436 | 22 | 98 | 79 |
| China, Yunnan-Fu | 25.2 N | 6371 | 24 | 91 | 42 |
| Sikkim, Manjitar, Rangit R. | 27.1 N | 818 | 51 | 95 | 175 |
| India, Cherrapunji (Assam) | 25.2 N | 4226 | 49 | 90 | 426 |
| India, Madras | 13.4 N | 22 | 57 | 113 | 48 |
| Taiwan, Keelung (Teipei) | 20.1 N | 33 | 37 | 92 | 135 |
| Burma, Mandalay | 21.6 N | 248 | 48 | 107 | 33 |
| Philippines, Baguio | 16.5 N | 4790 | 46 | 77 | 183 |
| Philippines, Manila | 14.3 N | 47 | 58 | 101 | 80 |
| Thailand, Bangkok | 13.4 N | 14 | 52 | 106 | 52 |
| Vietnam, Saigon | 10.4 N | 37 | 59 | 104 | 70 |
| Ceylon, Colombo | 6.5 N | 24 | 62 | 97 | 80 |
| Borneo, Sandakan | 5.5 N | 10 | 69 | 97 | 120 |
| Sumatra, Toba | 2.5 N | 3773 | 57 | 80 | 90 |
| Malaya, Singapore | 1.2 N | 8 | 66 | 97 | 95 |
| Java, Jakarta | 6.1 S | 26 | 66 | 96 | 72 |
| Java, Bogor | 6.6 S | 920 | 64 | 90 | 172 |
| New Guinea, Port Moresby | 9.3 S | 128 | 68 | 98 | 41 |
| **AUSTRALASIA** | | | | | |
| Hawaii, Honolulu | 21.2 N | 13 | 52 | 90 | 28 |
| Hawaii, Hilo | 19.4 N | 40 | 51 | 91 | 137 |
| Fiji Is., Suva | 18.8 S | 44 | 57 | 98 | 112 |
| Australia, Brisbane | 27.3 S | 137 | 36 | 109 | 45 |
| New Zealand, Auckland | 36.5 S | 152 | 32 | 90 | 44 |

Freezing point zero deg. Centigrade = 32 deg. Fahrenheit (F.).
1 meter (m) = 40 inches (or 3.28 feet).

# Guide to Care of Plants Indoors

## QUICK REFERENCE KEY TO CARE ( see chart on page 11 )

| HOUSE PLANT | GREENH. PLANT | WARM | TEMPERATE | COOL | SUN | FILTERED | NO SUN | LOAM | HUMUS | DRY | MOIST |
|---|---|---|---|---|---|---|---|---|---|---|---|
| 1 | 51 | W | | | S | | | L | | D | |
| 2 | 52 | W | | | S | | | L | | | M |
| 3 | 53 | W | | | | F | | L | | D | |
| 4 | 54 | W | | | | F | | L | | | M |
| 5 | 55 | W | | | | | N | L | | D | |
| 6 | 56 | W | | | | | N | L | | | M |
| 7 | 57 | W | | | S | | | | H | D | |
| 8 | 58 | W | | | S | | | | H | | M |
| 9 | 59 | W | | | | F | | | H | D | |
| 10 | 60 | W | | | | F | | | H | | M |
| 11 | 61 | W | | | | | N | | H | D | |
| 12 | 62 | W | | | | | N | | H | | M |
| 13 | 63 | | T | | S | | | L | | D | |
| 14 | 64 | | T | | S | | | L | | | M |
| 15 | 65 | | T | | | F | | L | | D | |
| 16 | 66 | | T | | | F | | L | | | M |
| 17 | 67 | | T | | | | N | L | | D | |
| 18 | 68 | | T | | | | N | L | | | M |
| 19 | 69 | | T | | S | | | | H | D | |
| 20 | 70 | | T | | S | | | | H | | M |
| 21 | 71 | | T | | | F | | | H | D | |
| 22 | 72 | | T | | | F | | | H | | M |
| 23 | 73 | | T | | | | N | | H | D | |
| 24 | 74 | | T | | | | N | | H | | M |
| 25 | 75 | | | C | S | | | L | | D | |
| 26 | 76 | | | C | S | | | L | | | M |
| 27 | 77 | | | C | | F | | L | | D | |
| 28 | 78 | | | C | | F | | L | | | M |
| 29 | 79 | | | C | | | N | L | | D | |
| 30 | 80 | | | C | | | N | L | | | M |
| 31 | 81 | | | C | S | | | | H | D | |
| 32 | 82 | | | C | S | | | | H | | M |
| 33 | 83 | | | C | | F | | | H | D | |
| 34 | 84 | | | C | | F | | | H | | M |
| 35 | 85 | | | C | | | N | | H | D | |
| 36 | 86 | | | C | | | N | | H | | M |

Explanations of the 5 elements combined in the

**PICTOGRAPH SYMBOLS**

used in this Manual

### Environment

⬜ = can be used as House Plant

⌂ = will do best in humid greenhouse

### Temperature

W = **WARM:** 62-65°F (16-18°C) at night; can rise to 80 or 85°F (27-30°C) in daytime before vents must be opened

T = **TEMPERATE:** 50-55°F (10-13°C) at night, rising to 65° or 70°F (18-21°C) on sunny day, or higher with air

C = **COOL:** 40-45° (5-7°C) at night, 55-60°F (13-15°C) when sunny, with air; 50°F (10°C) in cloudy weather

### Light *

= **MAXIMUM LIGHT, SUNNY:** Preference 4000-8000 ft.-candles; tolerance 500-2000 ft.-candles.

= **PARTIAL SHADE:** Preference 1000-3000 ft.-candles; tolerance 100-1000 ft.-candles.

= **SHADY OR AWAY FROM SUN:** Preference 50-500 ft.-candles; tolerance, as low as 10 ft.-candles.

### Soil

= **LOAM,** clay or good garden soil; humus added, peatmoss, or fibers

= **HUMUSY SOIL,** peatmoss, leafmold, or fibers

### Watering

= **DRENCH** thoroughly then allow to become dry

= **KEEP MOIST** but not constantly wet

---

\* 1 foot-candle = metric term 10.76 Lux.